INTRODUCING
ISSUES WITH
OPPOSING
VIEWPOINTS®

Nuclear Power

Lauri S. Friedman, *Book Editor*

GREENHAVEN PRESS
A part of Gale, Cengage Learning

GALE
CENGAGE Learning™

Detroit • New York • San Francisco • New Haven, Conn • Waterville, Maine • London

Christine Nasso, *Publisher*
Elizabeth Des Chenes, *Managing Editor*

For more information, contact:
Greenhaven Press
27500 Drake Rd.
Farmington Hills, MI 48331-3535
Or you can visit our Internet site at gale.cengage.com

For product information and technology assistance, contact us at

Gale Customer Support, 1-800-877-4253
For permission to use material from this text or product, submit all requests online at www.cengage.com/permissions

Further permissions questions can be emailed to permissionrequest@cengage.com

Articles in Greenhaven Press anthologies are often edited for length to meet page requirements. In addition, original titles of these works are changed to clearly present the main thesis and to explicitly indicate the author's opinion. Every effort is made to ensure that Greenhaven Press accurately reflects the original intent of the authors. Every effort has been made to trace the owners of copyrighted material.

Cover image copyright © Martin D. Vonka, 2009. Used under license from Shutterstock.com.

LIBRARY OF CONGRESS CATALOGING-IN-PUBLICATION DATA

Nuclear power / Lauri S. Friedman, book editor.
    p. cm. -- (Introducing issues with opposing viewpoints)
    Includes bibliographical references and index.
    ISBN 978-0-7377-4482-8 (hardcover)
    1. Nuclear engineering--Political aspects--Juvenile literature. 2. Nuclear energy--Environmental aspects--Juvenile literature. 3. Climatic changes--Prevention--Juvenile literature. 4. Radioactive wastes--Juvenile literature. I. Friedman, Lauri S.
    TK9148.N825 2009
    333.792'4--dc22
                                                                2009020985

Printed in the United States of America
1 2 3 4 5 6 7 13 12 11 10 09

Contents

Chapter 3: Could Nuclear Power Be Used for Terrorism?

Foreword

Indulging in a wide spectrum of ideas, beliefs, and perspectives is a critical cornerstone of democracy. After all, it is often debates over differences of opinion, such as whether to legalize abortion, how to treat prisoners, or when to enact the death penalty, that shape our society and drive it forward. Such diversity of thought is frequently regarded as the hallmark of a healthy and civilized culture. As the Reverend Clifford Schutjer of the First Congregational Church in Mansfield, Ohio, declared in a 2001 sermon, "Surrounding oneself with only like-minded people, restricting what we listen to or read only to what we find agreeable is irresponsible. Refusing to entertain doubts once we make up our minds is a subtle but deadly form of arrogance." With this advice in mind, Introducing Issues with Opposing Viewpoints books aim to open readers' minds to the critically divergent views that comprise our world's most important debates.

Introducing Issues with Opposing Viewpoints simplifies for students the enormous and often overwhelming mass of material now available via print and electronic media. Collected in every volume is an array of opinions that captures the essence of a particular controversy or topic. Introducing Issues with Opposing Viewpoints books embody the spirit of nineteenth-century journalist Charles A. Dana's axiom: "Fight for your opinions, but do not believe that they contain the whole truth, or the only truth." Absorbing such contrasting opinions teaches students to analyze the strength of an argument and compare it to its opposition. From this process readers can inform and strengthen their own opinions, or be exposed to new information that will change their minds. Introducing Issues with Opposing Viewpoints is a mosaic of different voices. The authors are statesmen, pundits, academics, journalists, corporations, and ordinary people who have felt compelled to share their experiences and ideas in a public forum. Their words have been collected from newspapers, journals, books, speeches, interviews, and the Internet, the fastest growing body of opinionated material in the world.

Introducing Issues with Opposing Viewpoints shares many of the well-known features of its critically acclaimed parent series, Opposing Viewpoints. The articles are presented in a pro/con format, allowing readers to absorb divergent perspectives side by side. Active reading questions preface each viewpoint, requiring the student to approach the material thoughtfully and carefully. Useful charts, graphs, and cartoons supplement each article. A thorough introduction provides readers with crucial background on an issue. An annotated bibliography points the reader toward articles, books, and Web sites that contain additional information on the topic. An appendix of organizations to contact contains a wide variety of charities, nonprofit organizations, political groups, and private enterprises that each hold a position on the issue at hand. Finally, a comprehensive index allows readers to locate content quickly and efficiently.

Introducing Issues with Opposing Viewpoints is also significantly different from Opposing Viewpoints. As the series title implies, its presentation will help introduce students to the concept of opposing viewpoints and learn to use this material to aid in critical writing and debate. The series' four-color, accessible format makes the books attractive and inviting to readers of all levels. In addition, each viewpoint has been carefully edited to maximize a reader's understanding of the content. Short but thorough viewpoints capture the essence of an argument. A substantial, thought-provoking essay question placed at the end of each viewpoint asks the student to further investigate the issues raised in the viewpoint, compare and contrast two authors' arguments, or consider how one might go about forming an opinion on the topic at hand. Each viewpoint contains sidebars that include at-a-glance information and handy statistics. A Facts About section located in the back of the book further supplies students with relevant facts and figures.

Following in the tradition of the Opposing Viewpoints series, Greenhaven Press continues to provide readers with invaluable exposure to the controversial issues that shape our world. As John Stuart Mill once wrote: "The only way in which a human being can make some approach to knowing the whole of a subject is by hearing what can be said about it by persons of every variety of opinion and studying all modes in which it can be looked at by every character of mind. No wise man ever acquired his wisdom in any mode but this." It is to this principle that Introducing Issues with Opposing Viewpoints books are dedicated.

Introduction

Nuclear power was once viewed as a very dangerous and unstable power source, one that had the potential to melt cities and kill thousands in just a few hours. Events like the 1986 Chernobyl nuclear accident in the former Soviet Union—in which a power plant malfunction released radioactivity into the environment, killing fifty-six and giving terminal cancer to as many as four thousand people—significantly undermined popular interest and trust in the nuclear industry.

But the twenty-first century has seen a reinvention of nuclear power as a safe, clean, green energy source. Concern over climate change has been a driving factor in nuclear energy's return to the forefront of the nation's energy agenda. As the United States and the rest of the world get increasingly nervous about whether fossil fuel use is contributing to a warmer planet, nuclear energy has emerged as a mighty fuel that can power the world as efficiently as fossil fuels but without emitting global warming gases such as carbon dioxide (CO_2). But what does it mean to be a "green" energy source, and does nuclear power count as one?

Compared with fossil fuels, nuclear energy delivers enormous amounts of power at very little cost to the environment. According to the Nuclear Energy Institute, nuclear power plants burn so cleanly that each year the world's 446 plants actually *prevent* the emission of 2.9 billion tons of CO_2 from burned fossil fuels into the atmosphere—and that number is expected to rise as more plants are built. In the United States alone, where 104 nuclear reactors provide 8.5 percent of the nation's total energy needs and nearly 20 percent of its electricity, it is estimated that nuclear power use avoids the release of 700 million tons of CO_2 annually—or the equivalent of taking more than 100 million cars off the roads. For this reason, nuclear power is an increasingly attractive energy option to those who think thwarting climate change should be a global priority.

Nuclear power has become billed as so green, in fact, that it has been embraced by environmentalists who once decried its use. Leading this pack is Patrick Moore, the cofounder of the environmental organization Greenpeace. Once vehemently opposed to nuclear power, Moore is now one of nuclear power's most enthusiastic proponents because he believes it offers the best way to save the planet from environmental disaster. "In the early 1970s when I helped found Greenpeace, I believed that nuclear energy was synonymous with nuclear holocaust, as did most of my compatriots," he explains. "Thirty years on, my views have changed, and the rest of the environmental movement needs to update its views, too, because nuclear energy may just be the energy source that can save our planet."[1]

But others argue it is not entirely appropriate to describe nuclear energy as a truly green energy source. For one, nuclear power generates toxic waste that remains dangerous for thousands of years. Although waste can be stored safely in holding tanks, these have the potential of leaking into the surrounding environment, causing cancer and birth defects. In this way nuclear power is quite different from other green energies like solar and wind power, which have few or no hazardous by-products.

A second reason nuclear power cannot really be put in the same category as solar or wind power is because it is not truly a renewable resource. Solar and wind power are renewable in that there is an infinite amount of wind or sun—provided the rays are shining and the breezes are blowing, humans cannot permanently use up these natural sources of energy. Yet nuclear power relies on a decidedly finite resource—the element uranium, which needs to be mined and processed in order for nuclear fission to take place. And like coal, natural gas, and oil, the earth only holds a certain amount of uranium and cannot make any more.

Different international organizations have a range of guesses for when the earth's supply of uranium will run out. The International Atomic Energy Agency has guessed supplies might last for another eighty years; the European Commission has guessed about seventy-two years; the Organisation for Economic Co-operation and Development and Nuclear Energy Agency have said supplies will last for at least another fifty years. While all of these estimates are greater than the projected amount of oil (which some experts guess might last another forty or so years), they cannot compete with the never-ending supply of sun and wind.

Furthermore, such guesses about the uranium supply are based on current consumption. But if the world were to increase its use of nuclear power as advocates recommend, the supply would be depleted even faster. According to the European Commission, for example, if nuclear power use increased sixfold, then a seventy-two-year projected supply would last just a short twelve years. It is for this reason that Paul Mobbs, author of the book *Energy Beyond Oil*, has said: "It would be unwise to advocate adopting the nuclear option when we have no realistic idea of how long the uranium resources will last. We would very quickly shift from shortages of oil and coal to shortages of uranium."[2]

It is difficult to say whether nuclear power's reinvention as a green energy source will be a passing fad or herald an energy revolution. Examining nuclear power's environmental impact is just one of the many issues explored in *Introducing Issues with Opposing Viewpoints: Nuclear Power*. Readers will also consider arguments about whether nuclear power pollutes, whether it is safe for humans, what to do with its waste, whether it is prone to terrorist attacks, and which countries should be allowed to produce it. Readers will examine these questions in the article pairs and conclude for themselves nuclear power's place in the coming energy future.

Notes

1. Patrick Moore, "Going Nuclear: A Green Makes the Case," *Washington Post*, April 16, 2006, p. B01. www.washingtonpost.com/ wp-dyn/content/article/2006/04/14/AR2006041401209.html.
2. Quoted in Angela Jameson, "Uranium Shortage Poses Threat," *Times* (London), August 15, 2005. http://business.timesonline .co.uk/tol/business/industry_sectors/industrials/article555314.ece.

Chapter 1

Is Nuclear Power a Green Energy Source?

Concern over climate change has brought nuclear power back to the forefront of discussions on alternative energy.

Viewpoint

1

Nuclear Power Is a Clean Energy Source

Patrick Moore

"Nuclear energy holds the greatest potential to arrest the dangers we face from global warming."

In the following viewpoint Patrick Moore argues that nuclear energy is a clean energy source that can help protect the environment and stave off global warming. Moore explains that the world is facing an environmental crisis, in part due to dangerous greenhouse gases that are emitted when fossil fuels are burned. Increasingly, it is argued that fossil fuels need to be replaced with alternative energy sources such as nuclear power. According to Moore, nuclear power is a non-greenhouse-gas-emitting power source. It does not release smog or other dangerous pollutants into the air. Yet at the same time, it is powerful enough to provide for America's energy needs. For all of these reasons, Moore urges Americans to start relying more on nuclear power for their energy needs.

Moore cofounded Greenpeace, an international group dedicated to protecting and conserving the environment. He currently serves as chair and chief scientist of Greenspirit Strategies Ltd. and as an adviser to the New York Affordable Reliable Electricity Alliance.

Patrick Moore, "Nuclear & Green," *New York Post,* February 23, 2007. Reproduced by permission.

As co-founder and former leader of Greenpeace [an international environmental protection and conservation group], I once opposed nuclear energy. But times have changed, and new facts of compelling importance have emerged—and so my views have changed as well, as have those of a growing number of respected, independent environmentalists around the world.

There are few places where nuclear power makes as much sense or is as important as in New York. Indeed, the state is a microcosm of the challenges America and the world face to have ample, clean and reasonably priced electricity. As such, I strongly support renewal of the license for the Indian Point nuclear plants in Westchester [New York], which provides 30 percent or so of the electricity used in the New York metro area.

Let me explain.

Nuclear Power Can Satisfy America's Energy Needs

Climate change is now high on the global agenda, and I believe nuclear energy holds the greatest potential to arrest the dangers we face from global warming. It is the only non-greenhouse-gas-emitting power source capable of effectively replacing fossil fuels and satisfying growing demand.

Hydroelectric is largely built to capacity. And while other key renewable energy sources will play a growing role, wind and solar power are unreliable and intermittent. They simply can't provide "baseload" electricity—especially in densely populated areas like downstate New York.

And with [New York City] Mayor [Michael] Bloomberg's 2030 Commission projecting the growth of the city's population by 1 million over the next few decades, New York's power needs can't be expected to shrink.

Worldwide, nuclear energy is one of the safest industrial sectors. Here in North America, no one has been harmed in the entire history of civilian nuclear-power generation. Indeed, it's proven safer to work at a nuclear power plant than in the finance or real-estate sectors.

Nuclear energy is already the No. 2 source of electricity in the United States; it accounts for nearly 30 percent of New York state's electricity.

Nearly 30 percent of New York state's electricity needs is supplied by nuclear power plants like this one in Buchanan, New York.

Nuclear Power Plants Improve Air Quality

Another environmental benefit: Nuclear power plants improve air quality by reducing smog.

Downstate New York arguably has the worst air quality of any region in the country, thanks to high levels of ozone and particulate pollution.

The five boroughs and four other New York counties—Nassau, Orange, Rockland and Suffolk—are in violation of both the U.S. Environmental Protection Agency's[1] ozone standards and its regulations on fine particulate matter.

It is well established that this pollution has harmful health effects, especially for children and the elderly. This needs to be addressed now.

Because of the many environmental and economic benefits, dozens of business associations, labor unions, community groups and others support Indian Point license renewal.

Nuclear Power Produces Little Waste

Nuclear energy also makes economic sense. The cost of producing nuclear energy in the United States is on par with coal and hydroelectric. That's a very important consideration in New York, which has the country's second-highest electricity costs. This impacts the poor and elderly, in particular, and makes it difficult for the business sector to operate efficiently as well.

What about nuclear waste? The notion is misleading. This used fuel is not waste. After its first cycle, spent fuel still contains 95 percent of its energy. Future generations will be able to put this valuable resource to work, powering the country.

---

1. An agency of the U.S. government charged with protecting human health and the environment.

Nuclear Power Around the World

Move than four hundred nuclear power plants provide 16 percent of the world's electricity.

	Operating Plants: Capacity MW (units)	Percent Nuclear Electricity Generation		Operating Plants: Capacity MW (units)	Percent Nuclear Electricity Generation
Argentina	2	7	S. Korea	20	45
Armenia	1	43	Lithuania	1	70
Belgium	7	56	Mexico	2	5
Brazil	2	3	Netherlands	1	4
Bulgaria	4	44	Pakistan	2	3
Canada	18	15	Romania	1	9
China	10	2	Russia	31	16
Taiwan	6	n/a	Slovak Rep.	6	56
Czech Rep.	6	31	Slovenia	1	42
Finland	4	33	S. Africa	2	6
France	59	79	Spain	9	20
Germany	17	32	Sweden	10	45
Hungary	4	37	Switzerland	5	33
India	16	3	Ukraine	15	49
Iran	—	—	UK	23	20
Japan	55	29	USA	103	19

World	442	16

Taken from: World Nuclear Association, "World Nuclear Power Reactors 2005–07."
www.world-nuclear.org/info/reactors.htm.

Nuclear Power Can Reduce Greenhouse Gas Emissions

Nuclear energy is not a silver bullet—it alone can't meet all of our energy needs. But the path toward cleaner air lies in the reduction of fossil fuels in favor of a mix of nuclear and renewable energy.

A growing consensus among environmentalists, politicians, industry and labor groups, academics and community leaders strongly supports a move in that direction.

Nearly 70 percent of Americans think more needs to be done to reduce greenhouse-gas emissions. I believe nuclear energy is well positioned to help achieve this goal and bring New York in line with the federal Clean Air Act [legislation that enforces the reduction of smog and air pollution].

The time for fresh thinking and renewed leadership on New York's energy needs is now.

EVALUATING THE AUTHOR'S ARGUMENTS:

The viewpoint you just read is written by the cofounder of the environmental group Greenpeace, which opposes nuclear energy. Does it surprise you that the author now supports the use of nuclear energy? What factors do you think might have caused him to change his mind, and do you think it is all right to switch positions on a topic like this? Explain your reasoning.

Nuclear Power Pollutes

Sherwood Ross

> *"Fuel rods at every nuclear plant leak radioactive gases or are routinely vented into the atmosphere by plant operators."*

Nuclear power pollutes the environment and is therefore not a green energy source, argues Sherwood Ross in the following viewpoint. When nuclear power is generated, nuclear fuel rods release dangerous radioactive gases that pollute the air and water. In addition, nuclear power leaves behind toxic waste products that do not break down for thousands of years. This waste is kept in holding tanks that can leak toxic chemicals into the environment. Furthermore, nuclear power relies on uranium and plutonium, both highly radioactive elements that are mined in environmentally unfriendly ways. Worse, mining for the uranium actually requires fossil fuels to be burned, which causes other pollution. The author concludes that nuclear power pollutes the environment in many ways and should not be considered a green energy source.

Ross is a Miami-based reporter and contributor to *Political Affairs*. He also hosts a blog on the Smirking Chimp, a liberal opinion Web site.

Sherwood Ross, "Nuclear Power Not Clean, Green or Safe," PoliticalAffairs.net, January 8, 2007. Reproduced by permission.

AS YOU READ, CONSIDER THE FOLLOWING QUESTIONS:
1. According to the author, what is burned during the mining and refining of uranium for nuclear power reactors?
2. What does the author say is contaminating the groundwater in cities in Tennessee, Ohio, and Kentucky?
3. Describe some of the symptoms experienced by Pennsylvania residents who were exposed to radiation during the Three Mile Island nuclear plant meltdown in 1979.

I n all the annals of spin, few statements are as misleading as [former] Vice President [Dick] Cheney's that the nuclear industry operates "efficiently, safely, and with no discharge of greenhouse gases or emissions," or [former] President [George W.] Bush's claim America's 103 nuclear plants operate "without producing a single pound of air pollution or greenhouse gases."

Nuclear Power Is Not the Answer

Even as the White House refuses to concede global warming is really happening, it touts nuclear power as the answer to it as if it were an arm of the Nuclear Energy Institute (NEI), the industry's trade group. NEI's advertisements declare, "Kids today are part of the most energy-intensive generation in history. They demand lots of electricity. And they deserve clean air."

In reality, not only are vast amounts of fossil fuels burned to mine and refine the uranium for nuclear power reactors, polluting the atmosphere, but those plants are allowed "to emit hundreds of curies of radioactive gases and other radioactive elements into the environment every year," Dr. Helen Caldicott, the antinuclear authority, points out in her book *Nuclear Power Is Not the Answer*.

What's more, the thousands of tons of solid radioactive waste accumulating in the cooling pools next to those plants contain "extremely toxic elements that will inevitably pollute the environment and human food chains, a legacy that will lead to epidemics of cancer, leukemia, and genetic disease in populations living near nuclear power plants or radioactive waste facilities for many generations to come," she writes. Countless Americans are already dead or dying as a result of those nuclear plants and that story is not being effectively told.

Nuclear Energy Produces Dangerous By-Products

To begin with, over half of the nation's dwindling uranium deposits lie under Navajo and Pueblo tribal land, and at least one in five tribal members recruited to mine the ore were exposed to radioactive gas radon 220 and "have died and are continuing to die of lung cancer," Caldicott writes. "Thousands of Navajos are still affected by uranium-induced cancers," she adds.

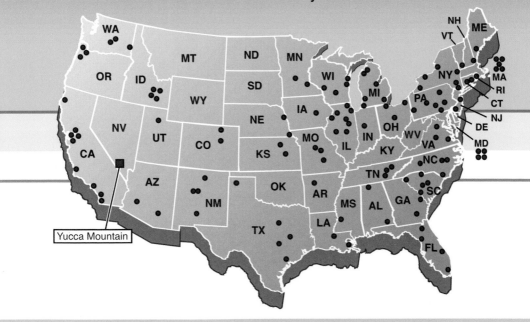

The Problem of Nuclear Waste

Nuclear waste is extremely toxic and takes thousands of years to decompose. Much of it is stored in containers that could leak or be attacked by terrorists.

Yucca Mountain

● Sites storing spent nuclear fuel, high-level radioactive waste, and/or surplus plutonium destined for geologic disposition

Taken from: U.S. Department of Energy, www.energy.gov.

As for uranium tailings [radioactive sand] discarded in the extraction process, 265-million tons of it have been left to pile up in, and pollute, the Southwest, even though they contain radioactive thorium. At the same time, uranium 238, also known as "depleted uranium,"(DU) a discarded nuclear plant byproduct, "is lying around in thousands of leaking, disintegrating barrels" at the enrichment facilites in Oak Ridge, Tenn.; Portsmouth, Ohio; and Paducah, Ky.; where ground water is now too polluted to drink, Caldicott writes.

Fuel rods at every nuclear plant leak radioactive gases or are routinely vented into the atmosphere by plant operators. "Although the nuclear industry claims it is 'emission' free, in fact it is collectively releasing millions of curies annually," the author reports.

Safety Standards Are Lacking

Speaking of safety, since the Three Mile Island (TMI) plant meltdown on March 28, 1979, some 2,000 Harrisburg [Pennsylvania] area residents settled sickness claims with operators' General Public Utilities Corp. and Metropolitan Edison Co., the owners of TMI.

Area residents' symptoms included nausea, vomiting, diarrhea, bleeding from the nose, a metallic taste in the mouth, hair loss, and red skin rash, typical of acute radiation sickness when people are exposed to whole-body doses of radiation around 100 rads, said Caldicott, who arrived on the scene a week after the meltdown.

> **FAST FACT**
>
> German scientists have found that when the environmental impact of mining uranium is considered, a 1,250-megawatt nuclear power plant produces the equivalent of 250,000 tons of CO_2 a year during its life.

David Lochbaum, of the Union of Concerned Scientists, believes nuclear plant safety standards are lacking and predicted another nuclear catastrophe in the near future, stating, "It's not if but when." Not only are such plants unsafe but the spent fuel is often hauled long distances through cities to waste storage facilities where it will have to be guarded for an estimated 240,000 years.

"The magnitude of the radiation generated in a nuclear power plant is almost beyond belief," Caldicott writes. "The original uranium fuel

A water-testing well sits on a section of land containing uranium tailings. The well monitors the level of radioactive waste on the site.

that is subject to the fission process becomes 1 billion times more radioactive in the reactor core. A thousand megawatt nuclear power plant contains as much long-lived radiation as that produced by the explosion of 1,000 Hiroshima-sized bombs."

Nuclear Plants Produce Too Much Waste

Each year, operators must remove a third of the radioactive fuel rods from their reactors as they have become contaminated with fission products. The rods are so hot they must be stored for 30 to 60 years in a heavily shielded building continuously cooled by air or water lest they burst into flame, and afterwards packed into a container.

"Construction of these highly specialized containers uses as much energy as construction of the original reactor itself, which is 80 gigajoules per metric ton," Caldicott points out.

What's a big construction project, though, when you don't have to pay for it? In the 2005 Energy Bill, Congress allocated $13-billion in subsidies to the nuclear power industry. Between 1948 and 1998, the U.S. government subsidized the industry with $70-billion of taxpayer monies for research and development, corporate Socialism pure and simple.

As for safety, an accident or terrorist strike at a nuclear facility could kill people by the thousands. About 17-million people live within a 50 mile radius of the two Indian Point reactors in Buchanan, N.Y., just 35 miles from Manhattan. Suicidal terrorists, Caldicott noted, could disrupt the plant's electricity supply by ramming a speedboat packed with explosives into their Hudson River intake pipes, where water is sucked in to cool the reactors. Over time, the subsequent meltdown could claim an estimated 518,000 lives.

Nuclear Power Is Not Clean, Green, or Safe

Caldicott points out there are truly green and clean alternative energy sources to nuclear power. She refers to the American plains as "the Saudi Arabia of wind," where readily available rural land in just several Dakota counties "could produce twice the amount of electricity that the United States currently consumes." Now that sounds clean, green, and safe. And I betcha it could be done through free enterprise, too. Somebody, quick, call in the entrepreneurs!

EVALUATING THE AUTHOR'S ARGUMENTS:

Sherwood Ross quotes almost entirely from one source to support the points he makes in his essay. Is it all right for an author to quote heavily from one source? Why or why not? Explain your reasoning.

Viewpoint

3

Nuclear Power Can Help Fight Climate Change

"The volume of greenhouse gas emissions prevented at the nation's 104 nuclear power plants is equivalent to taking 96 percent of all passenger cars off America's roadways."

Alex Flint

In the following viewpoint Alex Flint argues that nuclear power can help prevent climate change. Unlike fossil fuels such as coal, oil, and natural gas, nuclear power does not produce any greenhouse gases, which are considered to be the main cause of global warming. The author explains that these gases trap heat in the atmosphere, raising the earth's temperature and threatening life everywhere. Because fossil fuels produce large amounts of these gases when burned, replacing them with nuclear power, Flint says, can reduce the amount of greenhouse gases—and particularly carbon dioxide (CO_2)—that they emitted into the atmosphere. Flint concludes that in order to stop global warming, the world must rely more heavily on nuclear power.

Flint is senior vice president of governmental affairs at the Nuclear Energy Institute, an organization responsible for developing U.S. policy on the nuclear power industry. Formerly he served as staff director for the U.S. Senate Committee on Energy and Natural Resources.

Alex Flint, Statement Before the Select Committee on Energy Independence and Global Warming, March 12, 2008.

Chairman Markey, Ranking Member Sensenbrenner, Members of the Committee, thank you for the opportunity to testify on nuclear energy's significant role in reducing greenhouse gas emissions in today's electricity generation portfolio and the expanded role that it can play in the future.

The Nuclear Energy Institute [NEI] is responsible for developing policy for the U.S. nuclear industry on generic technical, regulatory, business and other matters of industry-wide importance. . . .

NEI's policy statement on climate change begins with the statement that "reducing carbon emissions, while fostering sustainable development, will be a major global challenge of the 21st century."

Electricity Demand Is Expected to Grow

The scope of that challenge was reinforced last week [March 2008] when the Administrator of the Energy Information Administration [EIA] testified before Congress on the EIA's 2008 Annual Energy Outlook. The EIA forecasts growth in U.S. electricity demand of 30 percent between 2006 and 2030. In large part, because the forecast also predicts the construction and operation of 16.4 gigawatts of new nuclear capacity, CO_2 emissions are predicted to increase by a smaller, yet still challenging, 16 percent from 2006 levels.

The global forecast is even more challenging. In 2030, world population is expected to be 8.3 billion people, an increase of 23 percent from today's estimated population. In addition, strong economic growth is forecast in the developing nations. To quote EIA, "total electricity demand in the non-OECD [Organization for Economic Cooperation and Development] nations is expected to grow from

2004 to 2030 at an annual rate that is nearly triple the rate of growth for electricity demand in the OECD."

Because of this rapid population and economic growth, EIA forecasts global electricity demand to nearly double between 2004 and 2030 from 16.4 trillion kilowatt-hours in 2004 to 30.4 trillion kilowatt-hours in 2030.

Nuclear Energy Is Necessary to Reduce Greenhouse Gases

It is extraordinarily challenging to imagine credible scenarios by which electricity production can double in the coming decades while reducing significantly the emission of greenhouse gases from electricity generation. To do so will take the successful implementation of a wide range of solutions. . . .

A credible program will require a portfolio of technologies and approaches, including the widespread use of nuclear energy, renewables, conservation, efficiency, and carbon sequestration from the use of fossil fuels. The magnitude of this challenge should not be underestimated.

Because of rapid population and economic growth, global electricity demand will double between the years 2004 and 2030.

That conclusion is shared by leaders and governments around the world including Yvo de Boer, Executive Secretary of the United Nations Framework Convention on Climate Change, who, in July 2007 said he had never seen a credible scenario for reducing emissions that did not include nuclear energy. Similar conclusions have been reached by the G-8 [an international forum of governments from eight nations] in its declaration on "Growth and Responsibility in the World Economy" issued after the June 2007 G-8 summit.

In addition to global policy leaders, the world's scientific community agrees that nuclear energy must play a significant role in meeting the dual challenges of electricity production and greenhouse gas reduction. The most recent UN scientific report on climate change, the Fourth Assessment Report of the Intergovernmental Panel on Climate Change [IPCC] identifies nuclear energy as one of the "key mitigation technologies." The IPCC report says that a "robust mix" of energy sources, including nuclear energy, "will almost certainly be required to meet the growing demand for energy services, particularly in many developing countries."

FAST FACT

The Office of Nuclear Energy reports that one ton of uranium produces more than 40 million kilowatt-hours of electricity, which can replace the equivalent of burning 16,000 tons of coal or using eighty thousand barrels of oil.

Strong Support for Nuclear Power

Business leaders concur. The World Energy Council's 2007 Energy and Climate Change Study found that "countries with high proportions of nuclear in their systems (such as Sweden and France) had GHG [greenhouse gas] emissions per head significantly lower (30–50%) than those of comparable nations, demonstrating the contribution nuclear could potentially make to dealing with climate change globally." The report recommends that "all governments should give serious consideration to the potential of nuclear power for reducing GHG emissions."

Similarly, the World Business Council for Sustainable Developments, in its *Powering a Sustainable Future* report, found that existing carbon-free

Greenhouse Gas Emissions Are Avoided by Nuclear Power Use

Nuclear power might be able to help reduce climate change. When used instead of fossil fuels, it keeps greenhouse gases—those that are believed responsible for global warming—out of the atmosphere. The following chart shows how much SO_2, NO_2, and CO_2 have been prevented from being released into the environment as a result of the use of nuclear power.

Year	Sulfur Dioxide (million short tons)	Nitrogen Oxides (million short tons)	Carbon Dioxide (million metric tons)
1995	4.19	2.03	670.60
1996	4.16	1.89	645.30
1997	3.97	1.76	602.40
1998	4.08	1.76	646.40
1999	4.13	1.73	685.30
2000	3.60	1.54	677.20
2001	3.41	1.43	664.00
2002	3.38	1.39	694.80
2003	3.36	1.24	679.80
2004	3.43	1.12	696.60
2005	3.32	1.05	681.92
2006	3.12	0.99	681.18
2007	3.04	0.98	692.71
Total	47.19	18.92	8,718.21

Taken from: Environmental Protection Agency, Energy Information Administration, and the Nuclear Energy Institute, May 2008.

technologies like nuclear energy and promising technologies including advanced nuclear energy, ". . . have the potential to contribute to the substantial decarbonization of the [electric] sector at acceptable cost by 2050."

In the United States, Dr. Jeffrey Sachs, the director of the Earth Institute at Columbia University has said "low-emission electricity generation will be achieved in part through niche sources such as wind and bio-fuels. Larger-scale solutions will come from nuclear and solar power."

The Progressive Policy Institute in its Progressive Energy Platform concluded "nuclear power holds great potential to be an integral part of the diversified portfolio for America. It produces no greenhouse gases, so it can help clean up the air and combat climate change. And new plant designs promise to produce power more safely and economically." . . .

Nuclear Power Benefits the Environment
The environmental benefit of this nuclear generation is substantial.

Nuclear power plants generate over 70 percent of all carbon-free electricity in the United States. By using nuclear power instead of fossil fuel–based plants, the U.S. nuclear energy industry prevented 681 million metric tons of carbon dioxide emissions in 2006. For perspective, the volume of greenhouse gas emissions prevented at the nation's 104 nuclear power plants is equivalent to taking 96 percent of all passenger cars off America's roadways. . . .

At a global level, 439 nuclear plants produce 16 percent of the world's electricity while avoiding the emission of 2.6 billion metric tons of CO_2 each year—and a new build renaissance is underway. . . .

The potential contribution nuclear power can make to reducing forecast greenhouse gas emissions in the electricity sector in the coming decades is extraordinary. But even as we work to build the next fleet of advanced reactors for electricity production, we also are developing reactors that will provide energy security and environmental benefits well beyond the traditional electric sector role. . . .

Nuclear Energy Can Combat Global Warming

In closing, nuclear energy is the single largest source of non-carbon emitting generation. It is a mature technology, operated at high standards by an experienced industry that is committed to safety. It is the only energy option available today that can provide large-scale electricity 24/7 at a competitive cost without emitting greenhouse gases.

EVALUATING THE AUTHOR'S ARGUMENTS:

Alex Flint quotes from several sources to support the points he makes in his essay. Make a list of everyone he quotes, including their credentials and the nature of their comments. Then analyze his sources—are they credible? Are they well qualified to speak on this subject?

Nuclear Power Cannot Help Fight Climate Change

Joseph Romm

"Nuclear power [isn't] likely to make up even 10 percent of the solution to the climate problem globally."

In the following viewpoint Joseph Romm argues that nuclear power cannot help fight climate change. For one, many more nuclear power plants would need to be built before nuclear power could make an impact on global warming. But these plants take a lot of money to build and operate. Furthermore, new plants take years to construct and would not be ready for at least another decade—but Romm says the world needs a clean, green energy source now. He also points out that the cost of nuclear power will be extremely high and likely lead consumers to other, more efficient energy sources anyway. For all of these reasons, the author does not consider nuclear power to offer a near-term solution to climate change.

Romm is the editor of Climate Progress, a project of the Center for American Progress Action Fund, which is dedicated to climate science, solutions, and politics. He is also a senior fellow at the Center for American Progress and a former assistant secretary

Joseph Romm, "Nuclear Bomb," Salon.com, June 2, 2008. This article first appeared in Salon.com at http://www.salon.com. An online version remains in the Salon archives. Reprinted with permission.

at the U.S. Department of Energy's Office of Energy Efficiency and Renewable Energy during the Clinton administration.

AS YOU READ, CONSIDER THE FOLLOWING QUESTIONS:
 1. Who is Michael Morris, and when does he predict the next nuclear power plant might be ready for use?
 2. What three forms of carbon-free power are cheaper than nuclear power, according to Romm?
 3. According to the author, what does nuclear power cost per kilowatt-hour before transmission and delivery costs are considered?

N o nuclear power plants have been ordered in this country for three decades. Once touted as "too cheap to meter," nuclear power simply became "too costly to matter," as the *Economist* put it back in May 2001.

Nuclear Power Has Too Many Problems

Yet growing concern over greenhouse gas emissions from fossil fuel plants has created a surge of new interest in nuclear. *Wired* magazine just proclaimed "Go nuclear" on its cover. Environmentalists like Stewart Brand and James Lovelock have begun embracing nukes as a core climate solution. And GOP [Grand Old Party, a nickname for the Republican Party] presidential nominee John McCain, who has called for building hundreds of new nuclear plants in this country, recently announced he won't bother showing up to vote on his friend Joe Lieberman's climate bill because of insufficient subsidies (read "pork") for nuclear power.

What do they know that scores of utility executives and the *Economist* don't? Nothing, actually. Nuclear power still has so many problems that unless the federal government shovels tens of billions of dollars more in subsidies to the industry, and then shoves it down the throat of U.S. utilities and the public with mandates, it is unlikely to see a significant renaissance in this country. Nor is nuclear power likely to make up even 10 percent of the solution to the climate problem globally.

Why? In a word, cost. Many other technologies can deliver more low-carbon power at far less cost. As a 2003 MIT [Massachusetts

Institute of Technology] study, "The Future of Nuclear Energy," concluded: "The prospects for nuclear energy as an option are limited" by many "unresolved problems," of which "high relative cost" is only one. Others include environment, safety and health issues, nuclear proliferation concerns, and the challenge of long-term waste management.

Too Expensive to Matter

Since new nuclear power now costs more than double what the MIT report assumed—three times what the *Economist* called "too costly to matter"—let me focus solely on the unresolved problem of cost. While safety, proliferation and waste issues get most of the publicity, nuclear plants have become so expensive that cost overwhelms the other problems. . . .

> ### FAST FACT
>
> According to the Nuclear Energy Information Service, the United States would have to construct 400 nuclear power plants to replace its coal-fueled plants. This would cost between $1.2 and $2 trillion and take several decades to enact. Meanwhile, CO_2 levels would continue to increase by 65 percent over the next thirty years.

After capital costs, wind power and solar power are pretty much free—nobody charges for the breeze and the sun. Operation is also cheap, compared with nukes, which run on expensive uranium and must be monitored minute by minute so they don't melt down. . . . The price of new nuclear power has risen faster than any other form of power, as a detailed study of coal, gas, wind and nuclear power capital costs by Cambridge Energy Research Associates concluded.

In fact, from 2000 through October 2007, nuclear power plant construction costs—mainly materials, labor and engineering— have gone up 185 percent! That means a nuclear power plant that would have cost $4 billion to build in 2000 would have cost more than $11 billion to build last October [2007]. . . .

At the end of August 2007, American Electric Power CEO [chief executive officer] Michael Morris said that because of construction

Construction and Cost of a Nuclear Reactor

Nuclear reactors take years to build and often end up exceeding their operating budgets.

Period of reference	Number of reactors	Average construction time (months)
1965–1970	48	60
1971–1976	112	66
1977–1982	109	80
1983–1988	151	98
1995–2000	28	116
2001–2005	18	82

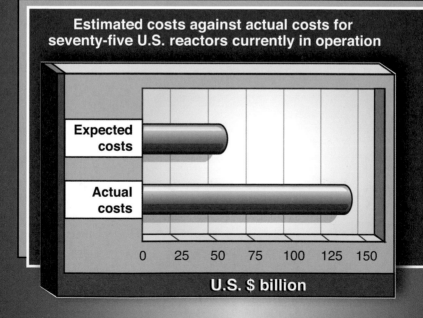

Estimated costs against actual costs for seventy-five U.S. reactors currently in operation

Expected costs

Actual costs

0   25   50   75   100   125   150

U.S. $ billion

Taken from: Greenpeace International, "The Economics of Nuclear Power," December 5, 2007.

delays and high costs, the company wasn't planning to build any new nuclear plants. Also, builders would have to queue for certain parts and face "realistic" costs of about $4,000 a kilowatt. "I'm not convinced we'll see a new nuclear station before probably the 2020 timeline," Morris said.

Critics of nuclear power point to a 2003 MIT study that concluded that the future of nuclear power is limited by high construction costs as well as many unresolved problems.

So much for being a near-term, cost-effective solution to our climate problem. But if $4,000 per kilowatt was starting to price nuclear out of the marketplace, imagine what prices 50 percent to 100 percent higher will do. . . .

Energy Efficiency Is Better than Nuclear Power

Many other forms of carbon-free power are already cheaper than nuclear today, including wind power, concentrated solar thermal power and, of course, the cheapest of all, energy efficiency. Over the past three decades, California efficiency programs have cut total electricity demand by about 40,000 gigawatt hours for an average 2 to 3 cents per kilowatt-hour. A May presentation of modeling results by the California Public Utilities Commission shows that it could more than double those savings by 2020.

If California's effort were reproduced nationwide, efficiency would deliver 130 gigawatts by 2020, which is more than enough energy savings to avoid the need to build any new power plants through 2020 (and beyond). And that means any new renewable plants built could displace existing fossil fuel plants and begin to reduce U.S. carbon dioxide emissions from the utility sector.

Nuclear Power Cannot Compete with Wind and Solar

A May [2008] report by the Bush Energy Department concluded that Americans could get 300 gigawatts of wind by 2030 at a cost of 6 to 8.5 cents per kilowatt-hour, including the cost of transmission to access existing power lines. And the cost of integrating the variable wind power into the U.S. grid would be under 0.5 cents per kilowatt-hour. (Wind turbines provide energy on average 35 percent of the time. Nukes average 90 percent availability. That means it takes 300 gigawatts of wind capacity to deliver as much electricity as about 120 gigawatts of nuclear.)

Finally we have the reemergence of concentrated solar thermal power (also known as concentrated solar power, or CSP). Utilities in the Southwest are already contracting for power at 14 to 15 cents per kilowatt-hour. The modeling for the California Public Utilities Commission puts solar thermal at around 13 cents per kilowatt-hour. Because CSP has large cost-reduction opportunities from economies of scale and the manufacturing learning curve, the modeling foresees the possibility that CSP costs could drop an additional 20 percent by 2020. And those prices include six hours of storage capacity, which allows CSP to follow the electric load, and that is even better than nuclear power, which is constant around the clock.

All of these sources of electricity are considerably cheaper than the electricity that would be generated by new nuclear plants, which the commission estimates costs more than 15 cents per kilowatt-hour before transmission and delivery costs. This entire discussion doesn't even consider the issue of uranium supply, whose price has risen sharply in recent years. A big shift toward nuclear power would no doubt further increase prices. If, as many advocates want, we ultimately go toward reprocessing of spent fuel, that would add an additional 1.5 to 3 cents per kilowatt-hour to the cost of nuclear power.

Nuclear Power Is Ineffective to Fight Global Warming

Sen. McCain keeps saying, "If France can produce 80 percent of its electricity with nuclear power, why can't we?" Wrong question, Senator. The right question is: Why would we? Energy efficiency and renewables are the key to affordable, carbon-free electricity. They should be a focus of national energy and climate policy. Not nukes.

> **EVALUATING THE AUTHOR'S ARGUMENTS:**
>
> In arguing against nuclear power, Joseph Romm focuses on cost. In your opinion, how important is the price of an energy source when considering its effectiveness? Is it worth it to you to pay more for certain sources of energy if they are particularly environmentally friendly or powerful? Why or why not?

Viewpoint 5

Nuclear Energy Is Better than Renewable Energy

William Tucker

> *"The energy stored in the nucleus of the atom is almost incomprehensibly larger than . . . the kinetic activity of wind, wave, or water."*

In the following viewpoint William Tucker argues that nuclear energy is far superior to renewable energy. Even though renewable energy sources like wind, solar, and hydropower have a reputation for being environmentally friendly, the author explains they take up huge swaths of land and produce relatively little energy. This is problematic, since land itself is a limited resource. Nuclear power, on the other hand, requires limited land to produce vast quantities of power. Tucker explains that the energy stored in the nucleus of an atom can go much farther than the energy produced by the sun, wind, or water. In fact, just 104 nuclear power plants currently provide nearly 9 percent of the nation's total energy. The author concludes that nuclear power puts far less pressure on the environment than renewable energy and should thus be considered the green energy of the future.

Tucker has written about energy and the environment for twenty-five years, with

William Tucker, "Food Riots Made in the USA," *The Weekly Standard*, April 28, 2008. Reproduced by permission.

articles appearing in *Harper's*, the *Atlantic Monthly*, and the *Weekly Standard*, to name a few. He is also the author of *Terrestrial Energy*, a book about how nuclear power will lead the green revolution.

AS YOU READ, CONSIDER THE FOLLOWING QUESTIONS:
1. What limited natural resource do all renewable energy sources depend upon, according to the author?
2. How much matter does the author say was needed to produce the energy unleashed by the nuclear bomb dropped on the Japanese city of Hiroshima in World War II? This is equivalent to how many tons of TNT?
3. According to the author, how often does a nuclear reactor require new fuel rods? In contrast, how much coal does a 1,000-megawatt coal plant need every day?

I n a position paper released only a few weeks ago [in the spring of 2008], the Natural Resources Defense Council, one of the many environmental organizations that has preached biofuels for decades, continued to insist that, "done right," ethanol can not only replace all our oil by 2050 but also "mitigate dangerous climate change."

Nice try, folks. Maybe U.N. [United Nations] officials don't eat raw corn, but livestock do, and that land could easily be used to grow crops for human consumption. As for the notion that homegrown ethanol can replace more than a tiny fraction of our oil consumption—let alone do anything to ameliorate world carbon emissions—that is an environmental hallucination. . . .

Biofuels Produce Little Energy

The Midwest has embraced this vision with a passion. One-third of the American corn crop will be converted to ethanol this year. Farmers are planting corn fencepost to fencepost and bringing new land under cultivation to cash in. The 51-cents-a-gallon federal tax credit assures a market. Ethanol distilleries are sprouting everywhere. Farm towns are revitalizing. The price of farmland is soaring. Presidential nominations turn on who supports ethanol in Iowa. Getting rid of this web environmental economist Timothy Searchinger of Princeton found that growing biofuels almost anywhere in the world will result in land being cleared somewhere else for food or fuel.

The *Science* articles have caused a biofuels meltdown. *Time*, which only two months ago [February 2008] was celebrating Richard Branson's conversion of one of his Virgin Atlantic jets to biofuels, ran an April [2008] cover story, "The Clean Energy Myth." It called biofuels "catastrophic" and "environmentally disastrous." . . .

Renewable Energy Depletes Land

Wind, hydro, and all the "alternate" sources of energy have been dubbed "green" because they are supposedly clean, renewable, and sustainable. In fact, what being "green" really means is that *they all require vast amounts of land.* In the beginning, when "alternate" efforts were still fairly modest, none of this much mattered. As they move up to industrial scale, however, the land requirements become staggering. And land, after all, is also a limited resource.

In a 2007 paper—well on its way to becoming a classic—Jesse Ausubel, director of the program for the human environment at Rockefeller University, calculated the amount of wood it would take to run one standard 1,000-megawatt electrical plant, the kind that can power a city the size of Cincinnati. Feeding the furnace year-round would require a forest of one thousand square miles. We have 600 such coal plants around the country now—to burn wood instead would require a forest the size of Alaska.

Other forms of stored solar energy make comparable demands. Glen Canyon Dam, which can produce 1,000 megawatts of electricity, is backed up by a reservoir 250 miles square (Lake Powell, in Arizona and Utah). That's why we stopped building dams in the 1960s—because they were drowning scenic canyons and displacing

of government intervention would now be just about as difficult as repealing farm subsidies in general.

So let's assess the damage. First, although biofuels have been anointed as clean, renewable, and sustainable, there has never been much evidence that they are producing *any* new energy. Growing crops consumes energy, and since only a small part of the plant—the seed—is distilled into alcohol, there's no guarantee of an energy gain. The most optimistic studies claim only a 25 percent energy profit, and some critics—David Pimentel of Cornell in particular—claim there is actually an energy *loss*. Suffice it to say, distilling one-third of our corn crop is replacing only 3 percent of our oil consumption. . . .

Biofuels Are Environmentally Dangerous

In February [2008], *Science* published an article by a team headed by Joseph Fargione of the Nature Conservancy showing that converting virgin land into ethanol cultivation multiplies carbon emissions by a factor of 93. "So for the next 93 years, you're making climate change worse," said Fargione. Another study in the same issue by

The author argues that solar and wind power production take up huge tracts of land that produce far less energy than a nuclear facility. Therefore, they are not environmentally friendly.

populations. (The 16,000-megawatt Three Gorges in China, probably the last major dam that will ever be built in the world, uprooted more than a million people.)

So it is with all forms of solar energy. Those 30-story windmills produce 1.5 megawatts apiece—about 1/750th the power of a conventional generating station. Getting 1,000 megawatts would require a wind farm 75 miles square. In a January [2008] cover story for *Scientific American,* three leading solar researchers proposed meeting our electrical needs in 2050 by covering southwestern desert with solar collectors. The amount of land required would be 34,000 square miles, about one-quarter of New Mexico.

And that's where biofuels went awry. Nobody ever bothered to calculate how much land they would require. . . .

Writing in the *Washington Post* in 2006, two former enthusiasts of biofuels, James Jordan and James Powell of Brooklyn's Polytechnic University, noted:

> It's difficult to understand how advocates of biofuels can believe they are a real solution to kicking our oil addition. . . . [T]he entire U.S. corn crop would supply only 3.7 percent of our auto and truck transport demands. Using the entire 300 million acres of U.S. cropland for corn-based ethanol production would meet about 15 percent of demand. . . . And the effects on land and agriculture would be devastating.

The extremely dilute nature of solar energy ensures that vast amounts of land will be necessary to capture and store it. Fossil fuels, on the other hand, may be bumping up against supply constraints and are creating environmental effects that will alter the earth's climate in unpredictable ways. So what other possibilities remain? . . .

More Energy than Renewables

The nucleus of the atom is the greatest storehouse of energy in the universe. The amount of energy released in the Hiroshima bomb was equivalent to 15,000 tons of TNT. Yet the amount of *matter* transformed into energy at Hiroshima was about 3 grams. If we are ever going to access enough energy to run our industrial economy without

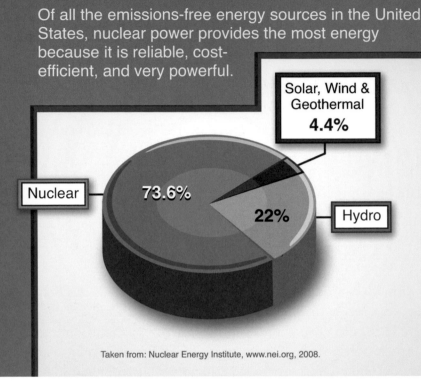

Sources of Emission-Free Electricity

Of all the emissions-free energy sources in the United States, nuclear power provides the most energy because it is reliable, cost-efficient, and very powerful.

Solar, Wind & Geothermal
4.4%

Nuclear — **73.6%**

22% — Hydro

Taken from: Nuclear Energy Institute, www.nei.org, 2008.

overwhelming the environment in the process, we are going to have to find it in the nucleus of the atom.

The energy holding together the nucleus of an atom is called "binding energy." When an atom splits in two—which happens occasionally in nature and can be induced in a nuclear reactor—some binding energy is liberated. This energy release is *two million times greater* than any "chemical" releases that come in, say, an internal combustion engine or a coal-fired electrical generating plant. This 2-million differential explains why a 1,000-megawatt coal plant must be fed by a 110-car train loaded with 16,000 tons of coal arriving *every day*. Meanwhile a nuclear reactor of the same size is fed by a single flatbed truck that arrives with a new set of fuel rods once every 18 months. The energy stored in the nucleus of the atom is almost incomprehensibly larger than the energy stored in fossil fuels or the kinetic activity of wind, wave, or water.

Atomic energy occurs naturally in the earth with the breakdown of uranium and thorium atoms. It is enough to heat the core of the planet to 7,000 degrees Fahrenheit and is the only form of energy that does not come from the sun. We could call it "terrestrial energy," to differentiate it from solar energy.

Nuclear Energy Is the Best Solution

Terrestrial energy is the answer to all the unpleasant questions raised by solar energy, which is why the nuclear industry in this country is poised for a comeback. Safety elements have been vastly improved, revamped plants are making enormous amounts of money, and the nuclear industry is chafing to start new construction. Although nuclear power cannot directly replace oil, it could become the basis of an expanded electrical grid that would support vehicles running on either electricity or hydrogen. It could end our energy odyssey. In light of last week's [April 2008] food riots and soaring world prices, it can't happen soon enough.

EVALUATING THE AUTHORS' ARGUMENTS:

In this viewpoint William Tucker argues that nuclear power is the only energy source that can provide enough energy to meet the demands of the U.S. industrial economy. How do you think the other authors in this chapter would respond to this claim? Write one sentence for each author.

Renewable Energy Is Better than Nuclear Energy

Arjun Makhijani

"Renewable energy sources are quite sufficient to provide ample and reliable electricity for the United States."

In the following viewpoint Arjun Makhijani argues that the United States does not need nuclear power plants to address climate change problems because renewable energy sources can be developed to reliably and economically supply all the electricity required. Furthermore, generating electricity with renewable energy is safer, less risky, and less costly than with nuclear power.

Makhijani is president of the Institute for Energy and Environmental Research, an organization that provides activists, policy makers, journalists, and the public with information on energy and environmental issues. Makhijani is also the author of *Carbon-Free and Nuclear-Free: A Roadmap for U.S. Energy Policy.*

AS YOU READ, CONSIDER THE FOLLOWING QUESTIONS:
 1. According to the author, how great is the wind energy potential of the Midwest and Rocky Mountain states?

Arjun Makhijani, "Nuclear Power, Not Renewable Energy, Is Risky Course for U.S.," *Deseret News* (Utah), February 10, 2008. Reproduced by permission.

2. According to the author, how many gallons of water would Utah's two proposed nuclear power plants consume daily?
3. What percent of U.S. electricity needs does the author say should come from renewable energy in the year 2025?

Given the seriousness of the climate crisis, many thoughtful people, including [Salt Lake City, Utah] *Deseret Morning News* Editor Joe Cannon, have argued that coal cannot be the source of our energy growth. I agree. He also advocated the revival of nuclear power as the mainstay of electricity growth amounting to 300 large power plants. This is risky, costly and unnecessary. Contrary to widely held opinion, renewable energy sources are quite sufficient to provide ample and reliable electricity for the United States.

Renewable Energy Is Plentiful

For instance, the wind energy potential of Midwestern and Rocky Mountain states is 2½ times the entire electricity production of the United States. Utah's neighbor, Wyoming, has almost as much wind energy potential as all 104 U.S. nuclear power plants combined. Solar energy is even more plentiful. The sunshine falling on rooftops and parking lots alone can provide much or most of the electricity requirements of the United States. Utah also has geothermal resources it can tap.

Renewable Energy Costs Are Competitive

Wind energy is already competitive with or more economical than nuclear energy—about 8 cents per kilowatt hour in very good areas. A recent independent assessment by the Keystone Center [a center for science and public policy], which included industry representatives,

Martin Roscheison, the CEO of Nanosolar, Inc., shows off the company's new solar panel that costs less than a dollar per watt to produce.

estimated nuclear costs at 8 to 11 cents. Intermittency is not a signifi-cant issue until very high levels of penetration. For instance, a 2006 study prepared for the Minnesota Public Utilities Commission found that an increase of just over 2 percent in operating reserves would be sufficient to underpin a 25 percent renewable energy standard sup-plied by wind.

Solar energy is somewhat more expensive today but costs are coming down rapidly. In December 2007, Nanosolar, a Silicon Valley company, produced the first solar panels costing less than a dollar a watt. When installed in megawatt chunks on commercial rooftops and commercial parking lots, the solar electricity is generated at the point of demand, avoiding the need for investments for major transmission lines, which can run into hundreds of millions or even billions of dollars. At an installed cost of $2 per watt, expected in the next few years, delivered parking lot solar energy cost will be 14 to 15 cents per kilowatt-hour. This is comparable to new nuclear plants at a delivered cost [of] 13 to 16 cents. Indeed, recent trends in solar costs indicate that nuclear power may become economically obsolete by the time the proposed nuclear power plants would come on line.

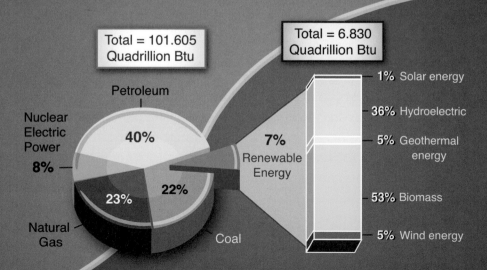

The Role of Renewable Energy

Renewable sources of energy account for more of the nation's total energy each year. Mandates requiring states to obtain a certain percent of their energy from renewable sources promise to increase their use in coming years.

Total = 101.605 Quadrillion Btu

Total = 6.830 Quadrillion Btu

Nuclear Electric Power 8%

Petroleum

40%

23%

22%

Natural Gas

Coal

7% Renewable Energy

1% Solar energy

36% Hydroelectric

5% Geothermal energy

53% Biomass

5% Wind energy

Note: Sum of components may not equal 100 percent due to independent rounding.

Taken from: Energy Information Administration, *Renewable Energy Consumption and Electricity Preliminary 2007 Statistics*, May 2008.

Renewable Energy Mandates in the United States

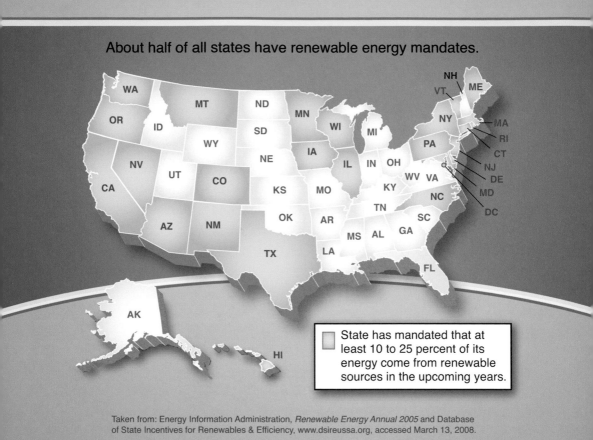

About half of all states have renewable energy mandates.

State has mandated that at least 10 to 25 percent of its energy come from renewable sources in the upcoming years.

Taken from: Energy Information Administration, *Renewable Energy Annual 2005* and Database of State Incentives for Renewables & Efficiency, www.dsireussa.org, accessed March 13, 2008.

Renewables Are More Reliable and Secure

Utah's existing hydropower and natural gas resources can be integrated with wind, solar energy and an efficient smart grid to provide reliable electricity. With the maturing of energy storage technologies, even coal-fired power plants can be phased out over a period of 30 to 40 years.

New nuclear plants would add to the country's mountain of nuclear waste, at a time when the federal government has long been in default of its obligations to existing nuclear plant operators to take the waste away from their sites. Utahns are already familiar with the desperate, and so far unsuccessful, attempts of some utilities to send their waste to a "temporary" storage site in the state.

Solar and wind do not need water. The two nuclear plants proposed for Utah would consume between 30 and 60 million gallons of water per day. The 300 plants that Mr. Cannon proposes nationally would consume over a trillion gallons of water per year at a time when water supply is becoming an uncertain resource. For instance, last September [2007], a nuclear unit at Browns Ferry belonging to the Tennessee Valley Authority had to be shut down for lack of water. Such problems can be expected to intensify in a warming world. A renewable electricity system would also be much more secure from terrorism than one that relies on nuclear power.

Renewable Energy Can Meet U.S. Electricity Needs

Last month [January 2008], MidAmerican Energy Holdings (which owns Rocky Mountain Power and is owned by Warren Buffet's Berkshire Hathaway), dropped plans to build a nuclear power plant in Idaho, on the grounds that it could not provide reasonably priced energy to its customers. Is that why some in Utah advocate an open checkbook for the nuclear industry to come and build a power plant, whatever the cost? If not the customers, then would taxpayers provide the subsidies?

The notion that renewable energy cannot supply the electricity requirements of the United States has been widely put forward without careful technical evaluation. On the contrary, it is nuclear that is the risky course. If the state of Utah is going to use its resources to encourage new electricity sources, a renewable portfolio standard of 25 percent by 2025 would help. And it could begin by installing solar panels on the parking lots and rooftops of its own buildings.

EVALUATING THE AUTHORS' ARGUMENTS:

In this viewpoint Arjun Makhijani explains that renewable energy is greener than nuclear power. The author of the preceding viewpoint, William Tucker, says that nuclear power is just as green as renewable energy. After reading both viewpoints, with which author's perspective do you agree? Why? Cite evidence from the essays you have read.

Chapter 2

How Dangerous Is Nuclear Power and Its Waste?

The nuclear reactor at Chernobyl, Ukraine, sits in a steel and concrete sarcophagus to seal it off from the world.

Viewpoint

1

Nuclear Power Poses a Serious Health Threat

Harvey Wasserman

"The radiation . . . spewed [from Chernobyl] still travels our jet stream, still lodges in our bodies, still harms our children."

In the following viewpoint Harvey Wasserman argues that nuclear power plants pose a serious health threat to humans. He claims that such plants emit dangerous levels of radiation, which is harmful to the human body. The health risk is even greater when power plant accidents occur. He uses the examples of the Chernobyl and Three Mile Island nuclear plant meltdowns to illustrate how nuclear radiation can cause death and sickness. In fact, residents in both areas experienced high rates of cancer, hair loss, bleeding sores, and asthma. In Wasserman's opinion, nuclear power is too dangerous to be used as an energy source and should be replaced with other sources of energy.

Wasserman is senior adviser to Greenpeace USA and the Nuclear Information and Resource Service. He owns Farmers Green Power Company, which works to create community-owned wind power. In addition, Wasserman has written or coauthored twelve books, including *Solartopia! Our Green-Powered Earth, A.D. 2030*, a futuristic novel about how green energy transforms the planet earth.

Harvey Wasserman, "Chernobyl Reminds Us That Nukes Are NOT Green," *The Huffington Post*, April 28, 2007. Reproduced by permission.

T wenty-one years ago this week [April 1986], lethal radiation [from the Soviet Union's nuclear-power plant Chernobyl] poured into the breezes over Europe and into the jet stream above, carrying death and disease around the planet.

It could be happening again as you read this: either by error, as at Chernobyl and Three Mile Island [TMI],[1] or by terror, as could have happened on September 11, 2001.

Those who now advocate a "rebirth" of this failed technology forget what happened during these "impossible" catastrophes, or refuse to face their apocalyptic reality, both ecological and financial.

The Failure of Atomic Energy

Radiation monitors in Sweden, hundreds of miles away, first detected the fallout from the blast at Chernobyl Unit 4. The reactor complex had just been extolled in the Soviet press as the ultimate triumph of a "new generation" in atomic technology.

The [Soviet] government hushed up the accident, then reaped a whirlwind of public fury that helped bring down the Soviet Union. The initial silence in fact killed people who might otherwise have taken protective measures. In downtown Kiev, just 80 kilometers away, a parade of uninformed citizens—many of them very young— celebrated May Day amidst a hard rain of lethal fallout. It should never have happened.

Ten days after the explosion, radiation monitors at Point Reyes Station, on the California coast, detected that fallout. A sixty percent

1. Location of a 1979 nuclear power plant accident in Pennsylvania.

drop in bird births soon followed. (The researcher who made that public was fired.)

Before they happened, reactor pushers said accidents like those at Three Mile Island and Chernobyl were "impossible." But. . . .

Nuclear Radiation Causes Disease and Death

To this day, no one knows how much radiation escaped from TMI, where it went or who it harmed. But 2,400 central Pennsylvanians who have sued to find out have been denied their day in court for nearly thirty years. The epithet "no one died at Three Mile Island" is baseless wishful thinking.

To this day also, no one knows how much radiation escaped from Chernobyl, where it went and who was harmed. Dr. Alexey Yablokov, former environmental advisor to the late [Russian] President Boris Yeltsin, and president of the Center for Russian Environmental Policy, estimates the death toll at 300,000. The infant death and childhood cancer rates in the downwind areas have been horrific.

A doctor takes blood for testing from a Ukrainian child with cancer. Even though the accident at Chernobyl occurred more than twenty years ago, people are still suffering and dying from its effects.

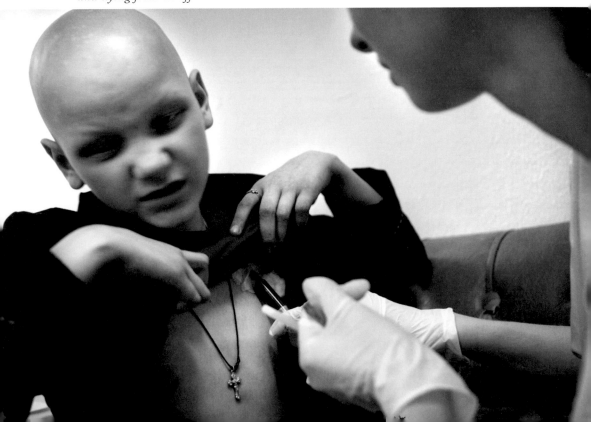

Visual images of the innumerable deformed offspring make the most ghastly science fiction movies seem tame.

Industry apologists have stretched the limits of common decency to explain away these disasters. Patrick Moore, who falsely claims to be a founder of Greenpeace, has called TMI a "success story." An industry doctor long ago argued that Chernobyl would somehow "lower the cancer rate."

FAST FACT

An April 2006 report by the European Greens for the European Parliament estimated there will ultimately be between 30,000 to 60,000 fatal cancer deaths as a result of the 1986 Chernobyl nuclear power plant accident.

In human terms, such claims are beneath contempt. As one of the few reporters to venture into central Pennsylvania to study the health impacts of TMI, I can recall no worse experience in my lifetime than interviewing the scores of casualties.

The farmers made clear, with appalling documentation, that the animal death toll alone was horrendous. But the common human symptoms, ranging from a metallic taste the day of the accident to immediate hair loss, bleeding sores, asthma and so much more, came straight out of easily available literature from Hiroshima and Nagasaki.[2]

There is no mystery about what happened downwind from TMI, only a conscious, well-funded corporate, media and judicial blackout.

At Chernobyl, the experience was repeated a thousand-fold. More than 800,000 (that's NOT a typo) Soviet draftees were run through the radioactive ruins as "jumpers," being exposed for 90 seconds or so to do menial clean-up work before hustling out. The ensuing cancer rate has been catastrophic (this huge cohort of very angry young men subsequently played a key role in bringing down the Soviet Union).

In both cases, "official" literature negating (at TMI) or minimizing (at Chernobyl) the death toll are utter nonsense. The multiple killing powers of radiation remain as much a medical mystery as how much fallout escaped in each case and where it went.

---

2. Japanese cities that were bombed by the United States during World War II.

Potential for Nuclear Accidents Is High

The economic impacts are not so murky. Moore's assertion that TMI was a success story is literally insane. A $900 million asset became a $2 billion clean-up job in a matter of minutes. At Chernobyl, the cost of the accident in lost power, damaged earth, abandoned communities and medical nightmares has been conservatively estimated at a half-trillion dollars, and still climbing.

The price of a melt-down or terror attack at an American nuke is beyond calculation. In most cases, reactors built in areas once far from population centers have now been surrounded by development, some of it bumping right up to the plant perimeters. Had the jets that hit the World Trade Center on 9/11/2001 instead hit Indian Point Units Two and Three, 45 miles north, the human and financial costs would have been unimaginable. Imagine the entire metropolitan New York

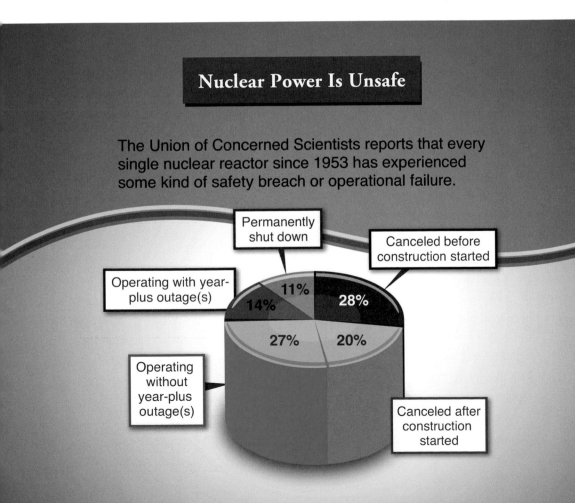

Nuclear Power Is Unsafe

The Union of Concerned Scientists reports that every single nuclear reactor since 1953 has experienced some kind of safety breach or operational failure.

Permanently shut down

Canceled before construction started

Operating with year-plus outage(s)

Operating without year-plus outage(s)

Canceled after construction started

11% 14% 28% 27% 20%

Taken from: Union of Concerned Scientists, www.ucsusa.org, March 12, 2008.

area being made permanently uninhabitable, and then calculate out what happens to the US economy.

There remains no way to protect any of the roughly 450 commercial reactors on this planet from either terror attack or an error on the part of plant operators.

Nuclear Power Emits Dangerous Radiation

Those advocating more nukes ignore the myriad good reasons why no private insurance company has stepped forward to insure them against catastrophe. Those who say future accidents are impossible forget that exactly the same was said of TMI and Chernobyl.

The commercial fuel cycle DOES emit global warming in the uranium enrichment process. Uranium mining kills miners. Milling leaves billions of tons of tailings [radioactive sand] that emit immeasurable quantities of radioactive radon. Regular reactor operations spew direct heat in to the air and water. They also pump fallout into the increasingly populated surroundings, with impacts on the infant death rate that have already been measured and proven. And, of course, there is no solution for the management of high-level waste, a problem the industry promised would be solved a half-century ago.

Economically, early forays into a "new generation" of reactors have already been plagued by huge cost overruns and construction delays. At best they would take ten to fifteen years to build, by which time renewable sources and efficiency—which are already cheaper than new nukes—will have totally outstripped this failed technology. Small wonder Wall Street wants no part of this radioactive hype, which is essentially just another corporate campaign for taxpayer handouts.

Nuclear Energy Equals Extinction

This past Earth Day [2007] was an orgy of corporate greenwashing, aided by the always-compliant major media, [which] tried to portray nukes as "green" energy. Nothing could be further from the truth.

We will never get to Solartopia, a sustainable economy based on renewables and efficiency, as long as atomic power sucks up our resources and threatens us with extinction.

Twenty-one years ago this week [April 1986], Chernobyl became something far worse than a mere warning beacon. The radiation it spewed still travels our jet stream, still lodges in our bodies, still harms our children.

Only by burying this failed, murderous beast can we get to a truly green future.

EVALUATING THE AUTHOR'S ARGUMENTS:

This viewpoint used dramatic descriptions to make its point that nuclear accidents like the ones at Chernobyl and Three Mile Island cause serious disease and death. Identify these dramatic elements and explain whether or not they helped convince you of the author's argument.

Nuclear Power Does Not Pose a Serious Health Threat

Iain Murray

> *"Cancer clusters appear all over the place, and are just as likely to appear next to an organic farm . . . as next to a nuclear facility."*

Iain Murray argues in the following viewpoint that nuclear power does not threaten human health. He complains that opponents of nuclear power perpetuate the myth that nuclear power plants are dangerous, emitting radiation that can cause sickness, cancer, and death. In reality, says Murray, nuclear power plants do not emit any higher level of radiation than that found naturally in the environment. In fact, all people are exposed to low levels of radiation on a daily basis, from both natural and human-made sources. As further proof that nuclear power is safe, Murray points out that employees of power plants and those living near them do not experience any higher incidences of cancer or death. The author concludes that nuclear power is safe and poses few health risks to humans.

Murray is a senior fellow at the Competitive Enterprise Institute, a nonprofit public policy organization dedicated to the principles of free enterprise and limited gov-

Iain Murray, "Nuclear Power? Yes, Please," *National Review,* June 16, 2008. Reproduced by permission.

ernment. He is also the author of *The Really Inconvenient Truths: Seven Environmental Catastrophes Liberals Won't Tell You About—Because They Helped Cause Them.*

AS YOU READ, CONSIDER THE FOLLOWING QUESTIONS:
1. According to the author, at what dose does radiation cause radiation sickness, cancer, and death?
2. How many cubic feet of nuclear waste does the author say Britain will have in the year 2040?
3. How much radiation would escape into the public from the proposed Yucca Mountain nuclear storage facility, according to the Department of Energy?

As to the safety of nuclear power stations, there is now a significant history to demonstrate that these concerns are no longer justified, even if they may have had some precautionary legitimacy in the 1970s. It has long been recognized that the Chernobyl accident[1] was caused by features unique to the Soviet-style RBMK (*reaktor bolshoy moshchnosti kanalniy*—high-power channel reactor). When reactors of that sort get too hot, the rate of the nuclear reaction increases—the reverse of what happens in most Western reactors. Moreover, RBMK reactors do not have containment shells that prevent radioactive material from getting out. The worst incident in the history of nuclear power, Chernobyl killed just 56 people and made 20 square miles of land uninhabitable. (The exclusion zone has now become a haven for wildlife, which is thriving.) There are suggestions that hundreds or thousands more may die because of long-term effects, but these estimates are based on the controversial Linear Non-Threshold (LNT) theory about the effects of radiation.

Low Doses of Radiation Do Not Cause Cancer
Official EPA [Environmental Protection Agency] doctrine, based on the LNT theory, holds that no level of radiation is safe, and that the maximum allowable exposure to radiation is an extremely stringent 15

---

1. A nuclear reactor accident at the Chernobyl Nuclear Power Plant in the Soviet Union in 1986.

millirems (mrem) per year. After Hiroshima and Nagasaki,[2] researchers discovered that 600,000 mrem was a sufficient dose of radiation to kill anyone exposed to it, and 400,000 mrem killed half the people exposed. Symptoms of radiation sickness develop at 75,000–

100,000 mrem. By extrapolating linearly, the model holds that there is no level of radiation at which someone is not adversely affected (hence "non-threshold"). Therefore, if a million people are exposed to a very low dose of radiation—say 500 mrem—then 6,250 of them will die of cancer brought on by the exposure. At least according to the theory.

But this is mere assumption, with no epidemiological evidence to back it up. As Prof. Donald W. Miller Jr. of the University of Washington School of Medicine wrote in 2004, "Known and documented health-damaging effects of radiation—radiation sickness, leukemia, and death—are only seen with doses greater than 100 rem [which is to say, 100,000 mrem]. The risk of doses less than 100 rem is a black box into which regulators extend 'extrapolated data.' There are no valid epidemiologic or experimental data to support linearly extrapolated predictions of cancer resulting from low doses of radiation."

Americans Are Exposed Regularly to Radiation

In fact, Americans are naturally exposed to around 200 mrem a year of background radiation. In some places around the world that background level is much higher. In Ramsar, Iran, thanks to the presence of natural radium in the vicinity, residents get 26,000 mrem a year, but there is no increased incidence of cancer or shortened lifespan. This is a real problem for the LNT theory. The predicted deaths and cancer cases haven't materialized.

2. Two Japanese cities where the United States dropped atomic bombs during World War II.

In Britain, much hay was made by Greenpeace and other organizations of the emergence of greater incidences of leukemia in children living near the nuclear-reprocessing plant at Sellafield in the early 1990s. But such "cancer clusters" appear all over the place, and are just as likely to appear next to an organic farm—to borrow the formulation of British environment writer Rob Johnston—as next to a nuclear facility. There does not appear to be any greater incidence of leukemia in the children of those who work in the nuclear industry.

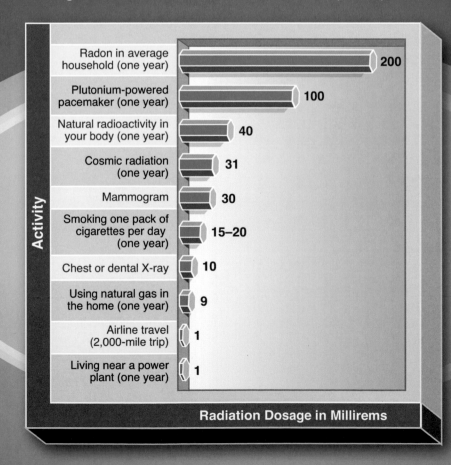

Radiation Risk from Reactors Is Low

Many natural and man-made sources of radiation pose a far greater risk to human health than nuclear power plants.

Activity	Radiation Dosage in Millirems
Radon in average household (one year)	200
Plutonium-powered pacemaker (one year)	100
Natural radioactivity in your body (one year)	40
Cosmic radiation (one year)	31
Mammogram	30
Smoking one pack of cigarettes per day (one year)	15–20
Chest or dental X-ray	10
Using natural gas in the home (one year)	9
Airline travel (2,000-mile trip)	1
Living near a power plant (one year)	1

Taken from: U.S. Department of Energy, Oak Ridge Office, "About Radiation," October 29, 2007.

In fact, there is so little evidence of significant safety risks related to nuclear power that the British government "continues to believe that new nuclear power stations would pose very small risks to safety, security, health and proliferation," according to a recent analysis it undertook. It also believes that "these risks are minimized and sensibly managed by industry."

Nuclear Waste Can Be Safely Managed to Protect Humans

Nuclear waste is a stickier problem, but one that can be safely managed. In most American reactors, fuel rods need to be replaced every 18 months or so. When they are taken out, they contain large amounts of radioactive fission products and produce enough heat that they need to be cooled in water. Radioactivity declines as the isotopes decay and the rods produce less heat. It is the very nature of radioactivity that, as materials decay, they become less dangerous and easier to handle. The question is what to do with the waste when space runs out.

According to the Department of Energy, the proposed nuclear waste storage site at Yucca Mountain would be safe and would not release harmful amounts of radiation into the atmosphere.

In most of the rest of the world, fuel reprocessing extracts usable uranium and plutonium. The highly radioactive waste that remains is not a large amount. By 2040, Britain will have just 70,000 cubic feet of such waste. This volume could be contained in a cube measuring 42 feet on each side. Moreover, most of Britain's waste is left over from its nuclear-weapons program. The British government has determined that "geological disposal"—burial deep underground—provides the best available approach to dealing with existing and also with new nuclear waste, arguing that "the balance of ethical considerations does not rule out the option of new nuclear power."

Exposure to Nuclear Waste Is Minuscule

In the U.S., unfortunately, reprocessing was stopped during the Carter administration, in the naïve belief that other countries would follow suit and thereby reduce the amount of plutonium available for weapons proliferation. For that reason, the U.S. has rather more nuclear waste than any other nation, about 144 million pounds of it. Since 1987, the U.S. has focused its own efforts at geological disposal at a remote Nevada site called Yucca Mountain, located within a former nuclear-test facility.

The story of Yucca Mountain is well-known—it has become a political football as pro- and anti-nuclear forces try to accelerate or delay (or even stop) the facility's commissioning. Legal challenges have focused on the question of how much radiation will escape to the public from the facility—over a timeline of a million years. The Department of Energy has calculated that exposure will be no more than 0.98 mrem per year, up to a million years into the future. Even those who hold to the stringent LNT view of radiation should be satisfied.

With that settled, the Department of Energy announced in 2006 that Yucca Mountain would open for business in 2017. But later that year, when Harry Reid was chosen as Senate majority leader, he announced, "Yucca Mountain is dead. It'll never happen." The project's budget has been slashed. As a result, the question of storing America's nuclear waste remains open, even as more and more of that waste piles up around the country.

No Scientific Evidence That Nuclear Power Is Dangerous

On the issue of persistence, bear in mind that reprocessing the fuel means that, after ten years, the fission products are only one-thousandth as radioactive as they were initially. After 500 years, they will be less radioactive than the uranium ore they originally came from. The waste question is therefore simply one of storage. It is a political, not a scientific, dispute.

EVALUATING THE AUTHORS' ARGUMENTS:

The author of this viewpoint argues that low levels of radiation produced by nuclear power do not lead to increased cancer or death in humans. How do you think the author of the preceding viewpoint, Harvey Wasserman, might respond to this argument? Explain your answer using evidence from the texts.

Nuclear Waste Can Be Safely Contained

Graeme Wood

"The most ridiculous fears surround the possibility that someone would seize any stored plutonium and use it to build a bomb."

In the following viewpoint author Graeme Wood argues that nuclear waste can be safely stored so it will not threaten life or the environment. Nuclear waste is made up of radioactive chemical elements left over from the process of nuclear fission, the force behind nuclear power. While these chemicals are dangerous, Wood says they can be safely stored in deep underground disposal facilities located in remote regions. These locations are secure and provide minimal exposure to people, keeping nuclear waste safe from potential theft or attack by terrorists. Furthermore, Wood explains that waste is kept in protective storage containers until it decays and is no longer dangerous. Instituting strict disposal standards will further help protect the environment from nuclear waste, he says.

Wood is a research and staff editor at the *Atlantic.*

AS YOU READ, CONSIDER THE FOLLOWING QUESTIONS:

1. How many tons of nuclear waste does the author say can be contained at the Yucca Mountain nuclear waste storage facility?
2. How long does it take for the worst of nuclear waste to decay, according to the author?
3. According to the author, what can leftover plutonium be used for?

T he [U.S.] Department of Energy is preparing to submit an application to the Nuclear Regulatory Commission for a license to store radioactive waste in Yucca Mountain, Nevada, under a plan endorsed by John McCain.

A Perfect Place for Nuclear Waste

The word "mountain" has lovely connotations: icy streams, conifer forests, unblemished views of a snowy sierra, yodeling competitions. (OK, so not they're not all lovely.) Alas for Yucca Mountain, these images of alpine sweetness do not apply to it at all. If Yucca Mountain had a name that conveyed just how baking-hot, barren, forlorn, and lifeless it is—perhaps "Yucca Death Vault" would do it justice—more people might see the logic in the government's plan, now nearly thirty years old, to use it to store the nation's radioactive garbage. The mountain is dry, geologically appropriate, and far enough from human settlements to keep it secure in case of accident or attack. Nevadans and anti-nuke activists object and say that the risk of leaks, of terrorist attacks, and of unforeseen catastrophes is too great to allow Yucca Mountain to accept the waste. But the waste has to go somewhere, and Yucca Mountain is the right spot.

> **FAST FACT**
>
> The U.S. Nuclear Regulatory Commission requires that high-level nuclear waste storage containers must maintain their integrity for three hundred to one thousand years.

Nuclear Waste Storage Is Safe

The alternative, first of all, is to keep the waste at the nuclear plants that produce it. Yucca Mountain is equipped to accept 77,000 tons of radioactive waste, which are currently *distributed all over the country*, often in areas near population centers. Few if any of the current nuclear plants could provide the security of a mountain in the middle of the country's most inhospitable and militarized desert.

Scientists, engineers, politicians, and lawyers have bickered for decades about whether Yucca is seismically inert enough to ensure

Nevada's Yucca Mountain is equipped to handle 77,000 tons of radioactive waste and is geologically stable and far enough from human settlement to be safe in case of an accident or attack.

millennia of safe storage. I don't blame skeptics for doubting. Storage beyond the scale of individual human lives, to say nothing of human history, is tricky and bound to pose risks, such as slow bleeds of radioactive waste into the ground or water. The good news is that the worst of the waste will have decayed significantly within centuries and the scariest parts of what's left—plutonium, which takes 24,000 years to decay by half—can be kept out of deep storage and instead reprocessed to power more reactors (or build bombs, about which more below). Now that storage and fossil-fuel costs are skyrocketing, this sort of reprocessing will make increasing economic sense, thereby reducing the period during which Yucca Mountain would have to be certified secure.

Nuclear Waste Not Easily Turned into Bombs

Finally, the subject of bombs: The most ridiculous fears surround the possibility that someone would seize any stored plutonium and use it to build a bomb. Let's assume a dramatic raid of Yucca Mountain actually did occur, and somehow the folks next door at Nellis Air Force Base were powerless to stop it. The terrorists would then have loads of fission fragments, plus a large quantity of the same material used to incinerate Nagasaki.[1] That improbable outcome would not be good, but it wouldn't be terrible, because contrary to its reputation, plutonium is neither all that dangerous nor all that difficult to get. It's not available, as Dr. Emmett Brown predicted over half a century ago, "in every corner drugstore," but nuclear power plants routinely produce the stuff as a waste product, and at last count there were nuclear plants all over the world, mostly not in the U.S. The trick isn't getting the plutonium, but turning it into a bomb. (Enriched uranium is the opposite—hard to find, easy to blow up.)

Yucca Mountain won't avert all catastrophes—whether of the bang or the whimper variety. But it will be better than the status quo.

EVALUATING THE AUTHOR'S ARGUMENTS:

In the viewpoint you just read, the author suggests that nuclear waste can be safely contained in underground storage facilities, thereby solving the problem of what to do with the waste created by nuclear energy. What do you think? Do you think this is the only way to handle nuclear waste, or can you think of a different solution? Explain your position.

1. One of two Japanese cities attacked by the United States with a nuclear bomb during World War II.

Nuclear Waste Cannot Be Safely Contained

Judah Freed

"No reasonable person can absolutely guarantee 100 percent safety and security along the hundreds or thousands of highway miles between current and future storage sites."

In the following viewpoint Judah Freed argues that nuclear waste is dangerous to humans and cannot be safely contained. He explains that nuclear power generates radioactive waste that takes thousands of years to decay, and there is no truly safe place in which to store it until it does. Storing it underground will contaminate the environment and drinking water and could threaten human life. In addition, Freed says it is impossible to protect nuclear waste from potential accidents or theft by terrorists. Freed concludes that since nuclear power is neither safe nor secure, government officials should turn their efforts to developing renewable energy sources.

Freed is a journalist, radio talk show host, and the author of *Global Sense: Awakening Your Personal Power for Democracy and World Peace.* He also writes a column for the Examiner.com.

Judah Freed, "McCain and Obama Both Wrong on Nuclear Power," Examiner.com, September 20, 2008. Copyright © 2008 Judah Freed. Reproduced by permission of the author.

CNN yesterday [September 19, 2008] released a fact check report proving another John McCain lie about Barack Obama. In this case, McCain claimed in a Michigan stump speech that he favors nuclear power while Obama is against it. In reality, CNN reported, the Obama-Biden New Energy for America Plan includes a section entitled "safe and secure nuclear energy."

If you visit Obama's website, as did CNN, you'll find in the plan this statement: "Nuclear power represents more than 70 percent of our non-carbon generated electricity. It is unlikely that we can meet our aggressive climate goals if we eliminate nuclear power as an option."

Obama's plan concedes, "before an expansion of nuclear power is considered," his administration would need to account for nuclear fuel and waste security, waste storage, and nuclear proliferation.

With due respect for senators Obama and McCain, they both are venting radioactive nonsense. Millions of lives are at stake, so let's dispel the absurd fantasy of "safe and secure" nuclear power. The only thing "green" about nuclear power is the money its backers hope to pocket.

Nuclear Waste Decays Slowly

We can start with the storage of nuclear waste from fission reactors.

The U.S. Government plans on storing nuclear wastes inside Yucca Mountain in Nevada from 2020 until 2133 at a total project cost of $96.2 billion in 2007 dollars, according to a Department of Energy study released in August [2008].

Before the Yucca Mountain facility goes into operation, the project must survive lots of lawsuits. Although litigation may end up before federal judges appointed by the Bush administration, which could skew the outcomes, if the cases are fairly tried on their merits, the facility may never start full-scale operations.

One of the strongest legal claims challenges the Energy Department assertion that the site will reach peak contamination in 10,000 years.

A train carrying radioactive waste snakes its way through France. The author contends that just one derailment could lead to disaster.

Opponents assert a more reliable scientific estimate, based on the 24,000-year half-life of plutonium, saying site contamination won't cease for at least 300,000 years. Will humanity still be living on our home planet by then?

Best Safety Precautions Are Not Enough

Another major legal challenge involves the Yucca Mountain storage facility being over a fault line. In the event of earthquakes, what would stop radioactive wastes from contaminating the underlying aquifer that supplies water for agriculture and urban populations throughout the West? Again, millions of lives are at risk, and this does not begin to count the peril to the Native Americans living nearby.

Even with the very best safety precautions, however, Yucca Mountain lacks the capacity to store all of the wastes now being stockpiled at more than 120 sites in the continental United States. If more nuclear power plants are constructed, as McCain and Obama intend, still more radioactive waste will have to be stockpiled without

THE NUCLEAR FAMILY: FATHER .. MOTHER .. 2·2 CHILDREN

www.caglecartoons.com

"The Nuclear Family: Father, Mother, 2.2 Children," cartoon by O'Farrell, *The Illawarra Mercury,* Australia, June 4, 2006. Copyright © 2006 by Vince O'Farrell, *The Illawarra Mercury,* Australia, and PoliticalCartoons.com.

Transporting Nuclear Waste Is Risky

If Yucca Mountain ever goes into operation, what about the safety and security of transporting all those wastes from their current storage sites to Nevada? Actually, this same concern applies to any other massive storage sites we might construct in any isloated part of the country we wish to make uninhabitable.

No reasonable person can absolutely guarantee 100 percent safety and security along the hundreds or thousands of highway miles between current and future storage sites. Traffic accidents are a danger, of course, and so are attacks or hijackings by nuclear terrorists. How many could die as a result?

If the shipments are sent by train, imagine the catastrophe from even one derailment, as happened recently with the non-nuclear toxic spill inside the rail tunnel under the English Channel. If the waste is transported by air, imagine the widespread contamination if an aircraft goes down or gets blown up. Again, how many could die as a result?

And what's to prevent theft? A fast search of the Web produced more than 30 fairly recent reports of radioactive materials being lost or stolen. In most of the reported cases, the loss was attributed to inattention or incompetence, yet other disappearances seem more sinister. What happens when there is much more nuclear materials available? Will more waste or spent fuel rods disappear? What if stolen nuclear materials are used to manufacture a bomb? . . .

Nuclear Power Will Never Be a Secure Energy Source

I say it's time we bust the myth of nuclear power ever becoming a "safe and secure" alternative energy source.

> **FAST FACT**
>
> According to Physicians for Social Responsibility, the United States has already accumulated more than 58,000 metric tons of highly radioactive waste at reactor sites throughout the country. There is no permanent repository for this waste.

Do not believe the propaganda from those with a financial interest in nuclear power. They see global climate change and rising petroleum prices as a chance to regain the public support lost after the 1979 Three Mile Island nuclear plant accident. In my opinion, they're trying to trick you.

Instead of spending many billions to build more nuclear power plants, instead of spending more billions to develop ways and means for securing all the additional radioactive materials these plants would produce, instead of spending billions to treat all those exposed to radiation when the inevitable accidents finally happen (or terrorist acts), let's spend those billions to develop sustainable sources of clean and renewable electrical energy.

I'd prefer we invest in improving the efficiency and lowering the costs of wind, solar and hydrogen fuel cell power. I'd prefer that we invest in battery technology breakthroughs. I'd also welcome a fresh infusion of capital into researching nuclear fusion, which would not produce the waste of nuclear fission.

As just one example of the options available, Managed Energy Technologies recently completed a proof-of-concept experiment for long-distance microwave transmission of electrical energy. Solar generators in geostationary orbit above the earth could transmit narrow beams of pure electrical power to earth-based receivers below. . . . That experiment only hints at the possibilities if we invest seriously in human ingenuity.

Nuclear Power Is Not the Answer

Given all of this, I urge both McCain and Obama to disavow support for building more nuclear-powered electricity generating plants. I urge both nominees to stop pandering to the "greenwashing" campaigns of the nuclear industry.

(I can say the same about both candidates' support for building more "clean coal" power plants, for that oxymoron is another misleading ploy to exploit the current energy crisis to deceive the public into backing pollution-prone technologies. However, we'll save that discussion for another day.)

If you really care about creating a sustainable future on our homeland earth, please visit both the Obama and McCain websites to send a message that you do not want any more nuclear power, that you want them to pledge support for a sensible, realistic energy plan that invests in genuinely clean energy technologies.

We can't afford to base our future on fatal fantasies.

EVALUATING THE AUTHORS' ARGUMENTS:

In this viewpoint Judah Freed explains that nuclear waste decays so slowly that it could contaminate a storage site for 300,000 years. The author of the preceding viewpoint, Graeme Wood, states that the worst of nuclear waste significantly decays within centuries. Why might their estimates be different? Which author provides better evidence to support his claim? Explain your reasoning.

Viewpoint

5

Nuclear Waste Can Be Safely Recycled

Donald J. Dudziak

"Spent fuel is not waste, but rather a valuable energy resource for the future."

In the following viewpoint Donald J. Dudziak argues that nuclear waste can be safely recycled. He admits that nuclear power plants produce a lot of waste, which is often stored on site because there is no safe place to put it. As such, nuclear waste is accumulating at power plants, making it vulnerable to theft and more likely to contaminate the environment. Dudziak suggests recycling this waste into new reactor fuel. He explains that uranium and plutonium, the elements responsible for nuclear power, can be extracted from spent nuclear fuel and used again to make new fuel. Recycling nuclear waste can also reduce nuclear weapons proliferation, preserve dwindling uranium reserves, reduce storage concerns, and provide a clean energy source that reduces global warming. For all of these reasons, the author supports recycling nuclear waste.

Dudziak is a fellow at Los Alamos National Laboratory, a science and technology institution that conducts multidisciplinary research in many fields, including national security, renewable energy, and medicine. He is also professor emeritus of nuclear engineering at North Carolina State University.

AS YOU READ, CONSIDER THE FOLLOWING QUESTIONS:
1. How much spent reactor fuel does the author say is currently stored at nuclear power plants?
2. According to the author, how can recycling nuclear waste reduce the spread of nuclear weapons?
3. How many jobs does the author say could be created if nuclear waste recycling facilities were built?

If the [George W.] Bush Administration and Congress want to focus energy policies more sensibly, New Mexico is the place to begin.

Thirty years ago, President Jimmy Carter put a halt to the recycling of spent fuel from nuclear power plants, on grounds that plutonium removed during the process might get into the hands of irresponsible governments or terrorists and lead to production of a nuclear weapon. Although President Reagan lifted the ban on recycling and other countries like France and Great Britain never stopped using the process, it was not resurrected in this country because recycling was considered too costly.

Uranium Should Be Recycled

Now that could change, given the growing importance of nuclear power in the battle against global climate change. In the United States, 17 utilities are preparing to build as many as 33 nuclear power plants. And here in New Mexico, a new uranium enrichment facility is under construction, and one or more nuclear power plants might be built. Worldwide, the number of nuclear plants is expected to double, with at least 1,000 operating by mid-century, but the likelihood exists there might not be enough uranium.

If the spent reactor fuel now stored at nuclear power plants in the U.S.—some 50,000 tons—were recycled instead of disposed of as nuclear "waste," it could be converted into new reactor fuel and

Time Line: U.S. Nuclear Waste Policy

1954 The Atomic Energy Act is passed by Congress. It gives the government the responsibility of disposing of highly radioactive waste.

1956 The National Academy of Sciences recommends deep geologic disposal of highly radioactive wastes from nuclear reactors.

1975 The Energy Research and Development Administration (ERDA) begins to search for a possible permanent repository for the nation's nuclear waste.

1980 Deep geologic disposal is selected by the Department of Energy as the preferred alternative for permanent disposal of commercial high-level nuclear waste.

1982 Congress passes the Nuclear Waste Policy Act of 1982.

1983 The Department of Energy (DOE) names nine previously screened potential repository sites in six states: seven in salt deposits and two on western federal nuclear facility sites (including the Nevada Test Site) in volcanic rock deposits.

1987 Congress amends the Nuclear Waste Policy Act, designating Yucca Mountain, Nevada, as the sole repository site to be studied for the permanent burial of 77,000 tons of high-level nuclear waste.

1988 DOE holds public hearings on its site characterization plan for Yucca Mountain.

1991 Surface studies begin at the Yucca Mountain site.

1992 Congress passes the Energy Policy Act, directing the Environmental Protection Agency (EPA) to develop site-specific radiation standards for Yucca Mountain.

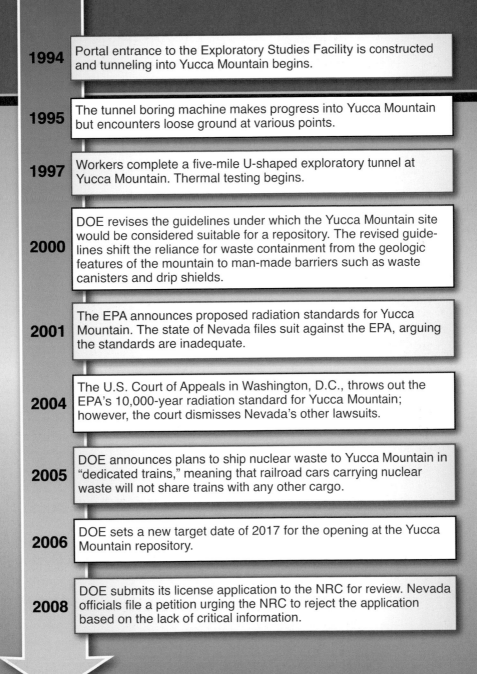

1994 Portal entrance to the Exploratory Studies Facility is constructed and tunneling into Yucca Mountain begins.

1995 The tunnel boring machine makes progress into Yucca Mountain but encounters loose ground at various points.

1997 Workers complete a five-mile U-shaped exploratory tunnel at Yucca Mountain. Thermal testing begins.

2000 DOE revises the guidelines under which the Yucca Mountain site would be considered suitable for a repository. The revised guidelines shift the reliance for waste containment from the geologic features of the mountain to man-made barriers such as waste canisters and drip shields.

2001 The EPA announces proposed radiation standards for Yucca Mountain. The state of Nevada files suit against the EPA, arguing the standards are inadequate.

2004 The U.S. Court of Appeals in Washington, D.C., throws out the EPA's 10,000-year radiation standard for Yucca Mountain; however, the court dismisses Nevada's other lawsuits.

2005 DOE announces plans to ship nuclear waste to Yucca Mountain in "dedicated trains," meaning that railroad cars carrying nuclear waste will not share trains with any other cargo.

2006 DOE sets a new target date of 2017 for the opening at the Yucca Mountain repository.

2008 DOE submits its license application to the NRC for review. Nevada officials file a petition urging the NRC to reject the application based on the lack of critical information.

Taken from: Eureka County Yucca Mountain Information Office, *Nuclear Waste Update*, Volume XIII, Issue 2, Summer 2008.

used again to provide clean electricity. This would help conserve the world's uranium resources.

Recycling Reduces Nuclear Waste

Another benefit from recycling is that it significantly reduces the volume, heat and toxicity of nuclear "waste," in effect more than doubling the capacity of the Yucca Mountain repository in Nevada. It means that Congress would not have to decide on a second or a third site for additional repositories after the first one is built. Equally important, the new recycling technology would never isolate the plutonium, thus greatly reducing weapon proliferation concerns.

The Department of Energy (DOE) plans to spend $250 million to demonstrate and deploy technologies for recycling, along with advanced reactors that can burn the recycled spent fuel. DOE's goal is to stimulate the use of nuclear power around the world, by assuring an ample supply of nuclear fuel, while limiting the risk of weapons proliferation.

Spent nuclear fuel is shown waiting for recycling as it sits in a storage tank at the Areva nuclear recycling plant in La Hague, France.

Nuclear Waste Is Not Useless

Known as the Global Nuclear Energy Partnership (GNEP), the DOE plan is to build and operate three facilities in the United States: one for recycling spent fuel and fabricating a mixed-oxide fuel for use in nuclear power plants to produce more electricity. Another facility would be an advanced "fast" reactor that would destroy long-lived radioactive elements while producing power. And a research facility would be used to develop new recycling processes and other advanced nuclear technologies.

So far, 11 sites around the country—including Hobbs and Roswell in New Mexico—have received DOE grants to conduct studies in order to determine whether they'd be suitable as locations for either the nuclear recycling center or the advanced reactor. Over the long term, the facilities are expected to require a capital investment of at least $16 billion, and bring in 8,000 jobs.

> **FAST FACT**
>
> The Global Nuclear Energy Partnership states that recycling nuclear waste into fuel for a new generation of reactors would produce one hundred times more energy than conventional reactors and generate 40 percent less waste.

The cost of developing new recycling technology would be stretched out over many years, so it will require an assurance of long-term, predictable funding for research, development and demonstration, involving universities and national laboratories.

No question about it, the idea of recycling is ambitious. It will entail perfecting a new technology for recycling, one that reduces the risk of weapons proliferation and is affordable. Also, a new generation of advanced nuclear reactors will need to be built.

Recycling Waste Is Safe

As we've learned well over the past 30 years, the absence of recycling and the unnecessary delays in opening the Yucca Mountain repository have placed nuclear power plants in the position of storing more spent fuel than expected, for longer than originally intended.

In reality, this spent fuel is not waste, but rather a valuable energy resource for the future.

We need to move forward with GNEP now. Otherwise, we could seriously limit the ability of nuclear power to provide the essentially emission-free energy that the world urgently needs.

EVALUATING THE AUTHOR'S ARGUMENTS:

The author of this viewpoint, Donald J. Dudziak, is a nuclear engineer, professor of nuclear engineering, and a fellow at Los Alamos National Laboratory, one of the largest science and technology institutions in the world. Does knowing the background of this author influence your opinion of his argument? In what way?

Nuclear Waste Cannot Be Safely Recycled

Robert Alvarez

"The key to recycling is being able to reuse materials while reducing pollution, saving money and making the earth a safer place. On all accounts, nuclear recycling fails the test."

Recycling nuclear waste is not safe for humans or the environment, argues Robert Alvarez in the following viewpoint. He claims that reprocessing plants—facilities where nuclear waste is recycled—release 15,000 times more radioactivity into the environment than a regular nuclear power plant. In addition, recycling uranium is highly ineffective because reprocessed uranium becomes more radioactive and more dangerous to work with and contaminates nuclear power plant equipment. Furthermore, the author explains that recycled plutonium is more easily stolen by terrorists and could be used to make bombs. For all these reasons, Alvarez concludes that the safety risks of recycling nuclear waste far outweigh any of its benefits.

Alvarez is a senior scholar at the Institute for Policy Studies, a nonprofit progressive think tank. He was also a senior adviser in the Department of Energy during the Clinton administration.

AS YOU READ, CONSIDER THE FOLLOWING QUESTIONS:
1. In Europe, what health risks have been created by reprocessing plants, as reported by Alvarez?
2. After trying for twenty-six years, what percent of the radioactivity found in nuclear waste does the author say the United States has successfully reprocessed?
3. What did the International Atomic Energy Agency conclude in 2007 about reprocessed uranium?

O ver the past few years, attention to the recycling of nuclear power spent fuel has grown. Fears of global warming due to fossil fuel burning have given nuclear energy a boost; over the next 15 years dozens of new power reactors are planned worldwide. To promote nuclear energy, the [George W.] Bush administration is seeking to establish international spent nuclear fuel recycling centers that are supposed to reduce wastes, recycle uranium, and convert nuclear explosive materials, such as plutonium to less troublesome elements in advanced power reactors.

Advocates, such as the Heritage Foundation, a conservative think-tank, argue that used fuel at U.S. power plants contains enough energy "to power every U.S. household for 12 years." Heritage points out that nuclear recycling "can be affordable and is technologically feasible. The French are proving that on a daily basis." . . .

The key to recycling is being able to reuse materials while reducing pollution, saving money and making the earth a safer place. On all accounts, nuclear recycling fails the test.

Nuclear Recycling Is Dangerous

In order to recycle uranium and plutonium in power plants, spent fuel has to be treated to chemically separate these elements from other highly radioactive byproducts. As it chops and dissolves used fuel rods, a reprocessing plant releases about 15 thousand times more radioactivity into the environment than nuclear power reactors and generates several dangerous waste streams. If placed in a crowded area, a few grams of waste would deliver lethal radiation doses in a matter of seconds. They also pose enduring threats to the human environment for tens of thousands of years.

In Europe reprocessing has created higher risks and has spread radioactive wastes across international borders. Radiation doses to people living near the Sellafield reprocessing facility in England were found to be 10 times higher than for the general population. Denmark, Norway, and Ireland have sought to close the French and English plants because of their radiological impacts. Discharges of Iodine 129, for example, a very long-lived carcinogen, have contaminated the shores of Denmark and Norway at levels 1000 times higher than nuclear weapons fallout. Health studies indicate that significant excess childhood cancers have occurred near French and English reprocessing plants. Experts have not ruled out radiation as a possible cause, despite intense pressure from the nuclear industry to do so.

Nuclear recycling in the U.S. has created one of the largest environmental legacies in the world. Between the 1940's and the late 1980's, the Department of Energy (DOE) and its predecessors reprocessed tens of thousands of tons of spent fuel in order to reuse uranium and make plutonium for nuclear weapons.

By the end the Cold War about 100 million gallons of high-level radioactive wastes were left in aging tanks that are larger than most state capitol domes. More than a third of some 200 tanks have leaked and threaten water supplies such as the Columbia River. The nation's experience with this mess should serve as a cautionary warning.

Cold War–era nuclear solid waste that polluted the Columbia River is shown dug up and awaiting cleanup on the Hanford nuclear reservation in Washington.

"How's your research on nuclear waste disposal going?"

According to DOE, treatment and disposal will cost more than $100 billion; and after 26 years of trying, the Energy Department has processed less than one percent of the radioactivity in these wastes for disposal. By comparison, the amount of wastes from spent power reactor fuel recycling in the U.S. would dwarf that of the nuclear weapons program—generating about 25 times more radioactivity. . . .

Fast Reactors Are a Failure

Recycling advocates . . . point to a new generation of "fast" reactors to break down plutonium so it can't be used in weapons. Since the 1940's, it was understood that "fast" reactors generate more sub-atomic particles, known as neutrons, than conventional power plants and it is neutrons which split uranium atoms to produce energy in conventional reactors. The U.S. actively promoted plutonium-fueled fast reactors for decades because of the potential abundance of neutrons, declaring that they held the promise of producing electricity and making up to 30 percent more plutonium than they consumed.

With design changes, fast reactors are, ironically, being touted in the U.S. as a means to get rid of plutonium. However, the experience with "fast reactors" over the past 50 years is laced with failure. At least 15 "fast" reactors have been closed due to costs and accidents in the U.S., France, Germany, England, and Japan. There have been two fast reactor fuel meltdowns in the United States including a mishap near Detroit in the 1960's. Russia operates the remaining fast reactor, but it has experienced 15 serious fires in 23 years.

Recycled Plutonium Is More Easily Stolen

Plutonium makes up about 1 percent of spent nuclear fuel and is a powerful nuclear explosive, requiring extraordinary safeguards and security to prevent theft and diversion. It took about 6 kilograms to fuel the atomic bomb that devastated Nagasaki in 1945. Unlike plutonium bound up in highly radioactive spent nuclear fuel, separated plutonium does not have a significant radiation barrier to prevent theft and bomb making, especially by terrorists.

Plutonium is currently used in a limited fashion in nuclear energy plants by being blended with uranium. Known as mixed oxide fuel (MOX), it can only be recycled once or twice in a commercial

> ## FAST FACT
>
> In 2006 research conducted by the environmental organization Greenpeace discovered radiation levels in groundwater in Normandy, France, that were 90 percent higher than European safety limits allow.

nuclear power plant because of the buildup of radioactive contaminants. According to a report to the French government in 2000, the use of plutonium in existing reactors doubles the cost of disposal.

The unsuccessful history of fast reactors has created a plutonium legacy of major proportions. Of the 370 metric tons of plutonium extracted from power reactor spent fuel over the past several decades, about one third has been used. Currently, about 200 tons of plutonium sits at reprocessing plants around the world—equivalent to the amount in some 30,000 nuclear weapons in global arsenals.

Recycled Uranium Is Highly Radioactive

In 2007 the International Atomic Energy Agency concluded that "reprocessed uranium currently plays a very minor role in satisfying world uranium requirements for power reactors." In 2004, about 2 percent of uranium reactor fuel in France came from recycling, and it appears that it now has dwindled to zero. There are several reasons for this.

Uranium, which makes up about 95 percent of spent fuel, cannot be reused in the great majority of reactors without increasing the levels of a key source of energy, uranium 235, from 1 to 4 percent, through a complex and expensive enrichment process.

Reprocessed uranium also contains undesirable elements that make it highly radioactive and reduces the efficiency of the fuel. For instance, the buildup of uranium 232 and uranium 234 in spent fuel creates a radiation hazard requiring extraordinary measures to protect workers. Levels of uranium 236 in used fuel impede atom splitting; and to compensate for this poison, recycled uranium has to undergo costly "over-enrichment." Contaminants in reprocessed uranium also foul up enrichment and processing facilities, as well as new fuel. Once it is recycled in a reactor, larger amounts of undesirable elements build up—increasing the expense of reuse, storage and disposal. Given these problems, it's no surprise that DOE plans include disposal of future reprocessed uranium in landfills, instead of recycling.

Recycling Nuclear Waste Is Impractical

As a senior energy adviser in the Clinton administration, I recall attending a briefing in 1996 by the National Academy of Sciences on the feasibility of recycling nuclear fuel. I'd been intrigued by the idea because of its promise to eliminate weapons-usable plutonium and to reduce the amount of waste that had to be buried, where it could conceivably seep into drinking water at some point in its multimillion-year-long half-lives.

But then came the Academy's unequivocal conclusion: the idea was supremely impractical. It would cost up to $500 billion in 1996 dollars and take 150 years to accomplish the transmutation of plutonium and other dangerous long-lived radioactive toxins. Ten years later the idea remains as costly and technologically unfeasible as it was in the 1990s. In 2007 the Academy once again tossed cold water on the Bush administration's effort to jump start nuclear recycling by concluding that "there is no economic justification for going forward with this program at anything approaching a commercial scale."

EVALUATING THE AUTHORS' ARGUMENTS:

The author of the previous viewpoint, Donald J. Dudziak, argues that recycling plutonium and uranium reduces the amount of radioactive material that could be stolen by terrorists. How does Robert Alvarez respond to this argument? Cite both texts in your answer.

Chapter 3

Could Nuclear Power Be Used for Terrorism?

Wearing protective gear, members of the Seattle Fire Department check for radiation during a nuclear "dirty bomb" terrorist response exercise in Chicago.

Nuclear Power Plants Could Be Attacked by Terrorists

Regina S. Axelrod

"Since September 11th, safety and terrorism at nuclear power plants continue to be major concerns."

In the following viewpoint Regina S. Axelrod argues that nuclear power plants are vulnerable to terrorist attack. Because nuclear power plants house deadly radioactive materials, she says terrorists are likely to be attracted to them—either to steal their dangerous materials or to turn entire plants into a fantastically devastating bomb. The plutonium and uranium used to make energy could be turned into bombs and other weapons. Or terrorists might hijack an airplane and crash it into a nuclear power plant. In addition to causing a massive explosion, radioactive gases would be released that could seriously harm or kill thousands of people. The author concludes that the world's stores of nuclear material need to be well secured so that terrorists cannot access the dangerous materials and wreak havoc on society.

Axelrod is a professor of political science and chair of the political science department

Regina S. Axelrod, "Radioactive Waste or Spent Nuclear Fuel; Reprocessing Pitfalls; Terrorism and Radioactive Material Transit; Nuclear Plant Safety; Conclusion," *Energy and the Environment: Why Nuclear Energy May Not Be the Answer,* April 26, 2007. Reproduced by permission.

at Adelphi University. She has published numerous articles and books on U.S. environmental and energy policy, including *Environment, Energy, Public Policy: Toward a Rational Future* and *Conflict Between Energy and Urban Environment.*

AS YOU READ, CONSIDER THE FOLLOWING QUESTIONS:
1. Why might terrorists be particularly likely to steal reprocessed plutonium, in Axelrod's opinion?
2. How many countries does the author say have reactors that hold enough enriched uranium to cause an explosion?
3. According to the author, what agency is responsible for defending nuclear power plants from terrorist attacks?

W hile nuclear energy is being marketed as the answer to the world's energy problems, serious problems with technology, safety and security issues, uncertainties surrounding licensing and financing and construction of new reactors, and the regulatory costs remain. . . .

Reprocessing Pitfalls

Reprocessing of spent nuclear fuel gives the appearance that something is being done to address the increasing amount of nuclear waste accumulating on site at nuclear power plants. Recycling is supposed to reduce the amount of waste that needs to be stored or disposed of there by extracting fuel for further uses; however, the by-product can be more toxic than the original waste. The plutonium that is separated out can be used to make nuclear weapons. It could be the target of terrorists because less radioactive plutonium can be more easily handled. The US and Germany abandoned their capability, although President [George W.] Bush has proposed to revive reprocessing (perhaps because of the frustrations over the problems associated with Yucca Mountain as the single US long-term repository). However, the costs are higher than mining for uranium and there is the potential for theft. Stolen radioactive material could be used with conventional explosives to make a dirty bomb. To eliminate this danger the US has removed spent fuel from reactors in Uzbekistan, Bulgaria, Latvia and the Czech Republic, sending it to Russia for storage. . . .

Creating a new waste stream of reprocessed plutonium could present new dangers and, contrary to common thinking, the total amount of nuclear waste isn't reduced unless it is continually reprocessed and reused: a process that has not yet been perfected. Even if it were, the government would incur a large financial responsibility overseeing the process. DOE [Department of Energy] Secretary Samuel Bodmen warned, ". . . [t]he stores of plutonium that have built up [in other countries] as a consequence of conventional reprocessing technologies pose a growing proliferation risk that requires vigilant attention.

Terrorism and Radioactive Material Transit

The prospects of terrorism at nuclear power plants, as well as, the consequences of an increase of nuclear waste and its transit around the world pose additional challenges. Even small amounts of radioactive material can be used to make a dirty bomb. . . .

The enriched uranium needed to make an explosion exists in reactors in 24 countries. . . . There are many opportunities where terrorists could gain access to radioactive material. . . .

Since September 11th, safety and terrorism at nuclear power plants continue to be major concerns. When the NRC [Nuclear Regularity Commission], conducted mock terror drills for certain nuclear power plants, security was breached and personnel were able to enter the plant and achieve their goal without the knowledge of plant officials and personnel.

The Indian Point nuclear power plant on the Hudson River, north of New York City, was under the flight path of one of the planes that crashed into the World Trade Center. There was pressure to institute a "no-fly" zone around the plant or in the proximity of it, but neither action has happened.

In the National Academy of Science report to Congress on "Safety and Security of Commercial Spent Nuclear Fuel Storage," it was concluded that spent fuel rods were a potentially successful terrorist

> **FAST FACT**
>
> According to Daniel Hirsch, president of the Committee to Bridge the Gap, nearly 50 percent of nuclear power plants in the United States have failed to prevent mock terrorist attacks during training exercises.

Security guards man their posts at the Three Mile Island nuclear power plant. Despite increased security following 9/11, many contend that such sites are still vulnerable to attack.

target and that an attack could lead to a fire that would release large amounts of radioactive material. The report also warned that a theft of spent fuel was also possible. The NRC refused to supply information to the committee writing the report, on measures taken to defend against attacks on spent fuel storage. It was concluded that theft and removal of fuel rod(s) was possible during an attack and remained a vulnerability. The report recommended that the NRC upgrade safety of spent fuel rods, analyze and address any insufficiencies that would lead to a fire and improve information-sharing including independent and public analyses between it and the nuclear industry. No agency is responsible for defending nuclear facilities against an attack such as on September 11th. The NRC and the nuclear industry claim it is not the responsibility of the NRC but the US government. However, the Department of Homeland Security and the Department of Transportation have yet to claim responsibility. . . .

Nuclear Plant Safety
. . .The NRC, so far, has not required utilities to submit new designs for nuclear power plants to ensure that the structures can withstand an

airplane attack. Utilities claim security is an NRC responsibility and therefore they are not required to make changes to existing plants or even future ones. According to the industry, simple and inexpensive changes could be made on-site to reduce vulnerability, e.g. having back-up generators on different sides of the facility.

Conclusion

. . . Cost is a significant factor in the decline of nuclear energy in the US in the 1970s and 1980s. Potential public opposition due to concerns about the safety and security of nuclear power plants and nuclear waste storage sites remains problematic. The lack of a permanent solution to the disposal of radioactive waste by any country may be the biggest hurdle for nuclear energy supporters. If new plants are built, tons of radioactive waste will continue to accumulate on plant sites. Moreover, the transit of this material to temporary above ground storage sites will pose additional security risks. Reprocessing can reduce nuclear waste but creates other problems. Such facilities could be used to produce nuclear weapons and the transit of radioactive material poses security problems because of accidents and terrorism. . . .

EVALUATING THE AUTHOR'S ARGUMENTS:

In the viewpoint you just read, Regina S. Axelrod describes how vulnerable nuclear power plants are to a terrorist attack. Given what you know on the topic, what ideas do you have for preventing terrorists from attacking a nuclear plant? Do you think there is any way to make nuclear power plants safe, or is this too dangerous an energy source to be used? Explain your reasoning.

Nuclear Power Plants Are Not Likely to Be Attacked by Terrorists

"There are 446 [nuclear power plants] worldwide. Not one has fallen victim to a successful terrorist attack."

Jack Spencer and Nicolas Loris

Nuclear power plants are not vulnerable to terrorist attacks, Jack Spencer and Nicolas Loris argue in the following viewpoint. They claim that most power plants are extremely well guarded, and even if terrorists were able to get around the tight security, it is unlikely they would be able to steal enough enriched uranium or plutonium to make a bomb. Spencer and Loris also dismiss fears of an attack by air or water as unreasonable, because since the attacks of September 11, airport security has improved so much that planes are unlikely to be hijacked and flown into targets. Furthermore, they point out that nuclear weapons are not able to be made from the materials housed at a nuclear power plant, so there is no danger of increasing the spread of nuclear weapons. Spencer and Loris conclude that fear of terrorism should not prevent the development of a potentially clean and efficient non–fossil fuel energy source.

Jack Spencer and Nicolas Loris, "Dispelling Myths About Nuclear Energy," Heritage Foundation Backgrounder, December 3, 2007. Reproduced by permission.

Spencer is a research fellow in nuclear energy, and Loris is a research assistant in the Thomas A. Roe Institute for Economic Policy Studies at the Heritage Foundation. The foundation is a think tank devoted to the principles of free enterprise, limited government, individual freedom, and traditional American values.

AS YOU READ, CONSIDER THE FOLLOWING QUESTIONS:
1. What is the "right response" to the threat terrorists pose to nuclear power plants, according to the authors?
2. How many nuclear materials shipments do Spencer and Loris say have been safely made since 1971?
3. According to the authors, how is making a nuclear weapon different from making nuclear power?

Anti-nuclear activists are reviving their fight against nuclear energy. On their Web site, NukeFree.org, the 2007 version of the old No Nukes movement warns of the catastrophic potential of nuclear reactors while advocating what they call safer, cleaner, renewable fuels, such as wind, solar, geothermal, and biofuels.

However, they ignore the reality that nuclear technology is a proven, safe, affordable, and environmentally friendly energy source that can generate massive quantities of electricity with almost no atmospheric emissions and can offset America's growing dependence on foreign energy sources. The arguments that they used three decades ago in their attempt to kill the nuclear industry were wrong then, and they are even more wrong today. A look at the facts shows that their information is either incorrect or irrelevant. . . .

Terrorists Have Never Attacked a Nuclear Power Plant

MYTH: Nuclear reactors are vulnerable to a terrorist attack.

FACT: Nuclear reactors are designed to withstand the impact of airborne objects like passenger airplanes, and the Nuclear Regulatory Commission [NRC] has increased security at U.S. nuclear power plants and has instituted other safeguards.

A successful terrorist attack against a nuclear power plant could have severe consequences, as would attacks on schools, chemical

German container trucks transport nuclear waste to recycling centers. Since 1971 more than 20,000 shipments of nuclear waste materials have been safely transported around the world.

plants, or ports. However, fear of a terrorist attack is not a sufficient reason to deny society access to any of these critical assets.

The United States has 104 commercial nuclear power plants, and there are 446 worldwide. Not one has fallen victim to a successful terrorist attack. Certainly, history should not beget complacency, especially when the stakes are so high. However, the NRC has heightened security and increased safeguards on site to deal with the threat of terrorism.

Nuclear Power Plants Are Well Protected

A deliberate or accidental airplane crash into a reactor is often cited as a threat, but nuclear reactors are structurally designed to withstand high-impact airborne threats, such as the impact of a large passenger airplane. Furthermore, the Federal Aviation Administration has instructed pilots to avoid circling or loitering over nuclear or electrical power plants, warning them that such actions will make them subject to interrogation by law enforcement personnel.

The right response to terrorist threats to nuclear plants—like threats to anything else—is not to shut them down, but to secure them, defend them, and prepare to manage the consequences in the unlikely event that an incident occurs. Allowing the fear of terrorism to obstruct the significant economic and societal gains from nuclear power is both irrational and unwise.

MYTH: Nuclear power results in nuclear weapons proliferation.

FACT: This claim is irrelevant inside the United States. Furthermore, manufacturing a nuclear weapon is wholly different from using nuclear power to produce electricity.

This myth relies on creating an illusion of cause and effect. This is why so much anti-nuclear propaganda focuses on trying to equate nuclear weapons with civilian nuclear power. Once such a spurious relationship is established, anti-nuclear activists can mix and match causes and effects without regard for the facts.

Furthermore, this "argument" is clearly irrelevant inside the United States. As a matter of policy, the United States already has too many nuclear weapons and is disassembling them at a historic pace, so arguing that expanding commercial nuclear activity in the United States would somehow lead to weapons proliferation is disingenuous. The same would hold true for any other state with nuclear weapons.

> # FAST FACT
>
> According to the Council on Foreign Relations, after the September 11, 2001, attacks the nuclear energy industry spent $1.25 billion to upgrade security at nuclear power plants throughout the United States.

As for states without nuclear weapons, the problem is more complex than simply arguing that access to peaceful nuclear power will lead to nuclear weapons proliferation. Nuclear weapons require highly enriched uranium or plutonium, and producing either material

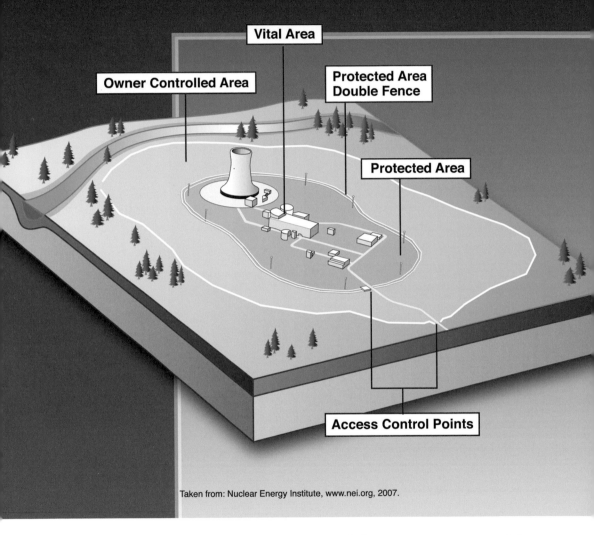

Nuclear Plant Security Zones

Nuclear power plants are protected by armed guards, physical barriers, and surveillance equipment.

Vital Area

Owner Controlled Area

Protected Area
Double Fence

Protected Area

Access Control Points

Taken from: Nuclear Energy Institute, www.nei.org, 2007.

requires a sophisticated infrastructure. While most countries could certainly develop the capabilities needed to produce these materials, the vast majority clearly have no intention of doing so.

For start-up nuclear powers, the preferred method of acquiring weapons-grade material domestically is to enrich uranium, not to separate plutonium from spent nuclear fuel. Uranium enrichment is completely separate from nuclear power production. Furthermore, nothing stops countries from developing a nuclear weapons capability, as demonstrated by North Korea and Iran. If proliferation is the concern, then proper oversight is the answer, not stifling a distantly related industry.

MYTH: Transporting radioactive materials exposes people to unacceptable risk.

FACT: The NRC and other regulatory agencies around the world take the strictest precautions when dealing with spent nuclear fuel. A staggering amount of evidence directly refutes this myth. Nuclear waste has been transported on roads and railways worldwide for years without a significant incident. Indeed, more than 20 million packages with radioactive materials are transported globally each year—3 million of them in the United States. Since 1971, more than 20,000 shipments of spent fuel and high-level waste have been transported more than 18 million miles without incident. Transportation of radioactive materials is just not a problem.

The NRC and other regulatory agencies around the world take the strictest precautions when dealing with spent nuclear fuel. The NRC outlines six key components for safeguarding nuclear materials in transit:

1. Use of NRC-certified, structurally rugged overpacks and canisters. Fuel within canisters is dense and in a solid form, not readily dispersible as respirable [capable of being inhaled] particles.
2. Advance planning and coordination with local law enforcement along approved routes.
3. Protection of information about schedules.
4. Regular communication between transports and control centers.
5. Armed escorts within heavily populated areas.
6. Vehicle immobility measures to prevent movement of a hijacked shipment before response forces arrive. . . .

Nuclear Power Plants Are Safe from Terrorists

Anti-nuclear activists successfully stopped the nuclear industry once before, but nuclear energy is too important to America to allow that to happen again. Despite the activists' attempts to mislead the public, nuclear energy is a proven, viable, economical, and environmentally sound solution to U.S. energy needs and legislative carbon constraints.

EVALUATING THE AUTHORS' ARGUMENTS:

Jack Spencer and Nicolas Loris argue that nuclear power plants are secure and safe and not likely to be attacked by terrorists. The author of the previous viewpoint, Regina S. Axelrod, disagrees. After reading both viewpoints, with which author do you agree? Use evidence from the texts to back up your answer.

Iran Should Be Allowed to Develop Nuclear Power for Peaceful Purposes

Stephen Zunes

"There is no evidence to suggest that Iran intends to use nuclear technology for purposes other than peaceful applications."

In the following viewpoint Stephen Zunes argues that Iran should be allowed to develop a peaceful nuclear power program. Zunes explains that the United States opposes Iran's development of nuclear technology because it fears Iran will use it to create nuclear weapons instead of electricity. But Zunes says there is little evidence that Iran is even capable of developing nuclear weapons. In fact, Iran has had a nuclear program for more than fifty years and has yet to use nuclear power for nonpeaceful purposes. Furthermore, Iran signed the Nuclear Nonproliferation Treaty, and therefore has as much right as other countries to develop nuclear energy for civilian purposes. The author concludes that Iran should not be singled out for

Stephen Zunes, "The Iranian Nuclear Threat: Myth and Reality," *Tikkun*, vol. 22, January/February 2007, pp. 29–32. Copyright © 2007 Institute for Labor and Mental Health. Reproduced by permission of *Tikkun: A Bimonthly Jewish Critique of Politics, Culture & Society.*

developing nuclear technology, nor should it be unfairly banned from developing a peaceful program alongside other nations.

Zunes is a professor of politics at the University of San Francisco and serves on the advisory board of the Tikkun Community, an interfaith community dedicated to achieving social justice, sound ecological practices, and world peace. Zunes is also the author of *Tinderbox: U.S. Middle East Policy and the Roots of Terrorism.*

AS YOU READ, CONSIDER THE FOLLOWING QUESTIONS:
1. According to the author, in what year did Iran develop its nuclear program?
2. What country does the author say is the only country to have used nuclear weapons in combat?
3. What lesson does Zunes suggest Iran might have learned from the United States' relationship with Iraq and North Korea?

There is a frightening sense of deja vu: Talk of the United States using military force against a Middle Eastern state with a nuclear program that allegedly poses a threat to the U.S. and the global community, and which also happens to sit on one of the world's largest reserves of oil.

Unlike Iraq in 2003, however, Iran really does have a nuclear program. While there is no evidence to suggest that Iran intends to use nuclear technology for purposes other than peaceful applications, concerns that the current civilian program could be a cover for a nuclear weapons development are not unfounded. Underlying these apprehensions is the fact that nuclear power is an unnecessarily expensive and dangerous means of electrical generation for any country, particularly one that is well endowed with other energy resources.

Iran's Nuclear Program Is Legal

However, developing nuclear power for civilian purposes is legal under the Nuclear Nonproliferation Treaty (NPT), which has been signed and ratified by Iran, the United States, and all but a handful of the world's nations. Iran is currently not doing anything that goes beyond what dozens of other signatories of the NPT are doing legally. Nevertheless, the United Nations' International Atomic Energy Agency (IAEA) has determined that Iran, by failing to report nuclear research activities back in the 1990s, had forfeited many of the rights afforded to other nations in regard to its nuclear development, such as enriching uranium—a restriction that Iran has rejected and has been violating for the past year [2006].

More than likely, Iran has not yet mastered the technique for turning uranium into uranium gas, which is necessary to reproduce highly enriched uranium. In addition, Iran does not have nearly enough centrifuges to enrich the uranium, either for fuel rods or for weapons, nor has Iran demonstrated the ability to operate cascades of centrifuges on a large scale. Finally, there is no evidence that Iran has developed a design of a missile re-entry vehicle that could carry a nuclear warhead. Indeed, Iran is unlikely to have a single deployable nuclear warhead until at least the year 2015.

In other words, there is plenty of time for a diplomatic solution.

Iran's Uranium Conversion Facility is seen shortly after construction was completed. The facility will produce uranium fuel for a nuclear reactor.

The United States Helped Iran Build Its Weapons Program

Despite the alleged urgency of this so-called crisis, it is important to note that Iran has had a nuclear program since 1957, when President Dwight Eisenhower signed the first of a series of nuclear cooperation agreement with the Shah, a brutal dictator installed by the CIA following its overthrow of the democratic government of Prime Minister Mohammed Mossadegh four years earlier. Over the next two decades, the United States not only provided Iran with technical assistance, but also supplied the country with its first experimental nuclear reactor, complete with enriched uranium and plutonium with fissile isotopes. Despite the refusal of the Shah to rule out the possibility of Iran developing nuclear weapons, the [Gerald] Ford administration in 1975 approved the sale of up to eight nuclear reactors with fuel, and in 1976, approved the sale of lasers believed to be capable of enriching uranium.

The *Washington Post* reported that an initially hesitant President Ford was assured by his advisors that Iran was only interested in the peaceful uses of nuclear energy. Ironically, these advisors were none other than his secretary of defense Donald Rumsfeld, his chief of staff Dick Cheney, and the director of nonproliferation at the Arms Control and Disarmament Agency, Paul Wolfowitz—the very advisors of the current [George W. Bush] administration who have been so alarmist about Iran's nuclear program.

Even if Iran aspires to build nuclear weapons, it would be a mistake to assume that the Islamic Republic would use them for aggressive designs. Indeed, the Iranians may have good reasons to desire a nuclear deterrent.

Iran Needs a Nuclear Deterrent

In early 2002, Iran was among three countries (the others being Iraq and North Korea) labeled by President George W. Bush as part of "the axis of evil." Iraq, which had given up its nuclear program over

Iran's Nuclear Facilities

Iran claims it seeks nuclear technology for peaceful purposes, such as the generation of electricity.

Taken from: Greenpeace, "An Overview of Nuclear Facilities in Iran, Israel, and Turkey," February 2007.

a decade earlier and subsequently allowed IAEA inspectors back in the country to verify the absence of such a program, was invaded and occupied by the United States. By contrast, North Korea—which reneged on its agreement and has apparently resumed production of nuclear weapons—has not been invaded. The Iranians may see a lesson in that.

Soon after coming to office, the Bush administration decided to unfreeze America's nuclear weapons production and launch a program to develop smaller tactical nuclear weapons for battlefield use. This fact was noted by many foreign states, including potential adversaries such as Iran. In this light, it is important to remember that the only country to actually use nuclear weapons in combat is the United States, in the 1945 bombings of two Japanese cities, a decision that most American political leaders still defend to this day.

Furthermore, the U.S. government is allied with Pakistan, which borders Iran to the east, and possesses nuclear weapons and sophisticated delivery systems. The U.S. is also a strong ally of Israel, located just 600 miles to Iran's west, which has the capability of launching, with long-range missiles, a nuclear strike against the Gulf state in a matter of minutes. . . .

U.S. Double Standards Are Unethical

The Bush administration . . . [insists] that the United States has the right to decide which countries get to have such weapons and which ones do not, effectively demanding a kind of nuclear apartheid.

Not only are such double standards unethical, they are simply unworkable: any effort by America to impose a hierarchy of haves and have-nots in the region would simply fuel rebellion from the have-nots.

The only realistic means of curbing the threat of nuclear proliferation in the Middle East is to establish a law-based, region-wide program for disarmament, by which all countries—regardless of their relations with the United States—must abide.

And, ultimately, the only way to make the world completely safe from the threat of nuclear weapons is for the establishment of a nuclear-free planet, in which the United States—as the largest nuclear power—must take the lead.

EVALUATING THE AUTHOR'S ARGUMENTS:

In the viewpoint you just read, Stephen Zunes suggests that Iran should be allowed to freely develop a peaceful nuclear program without the threat of military force by the United States. What do you think? Should Iran be treated any differently from any other nation developing nuclear programs? Why or why not? Explain your position.

Viewpoint

4

Iran Does Not Intend to Develop Nuclear Power for Peaceful Purposes

"Iran's claim that its nuclear program is for electricity production appears doubtful in light of its large oil and natural gas reserves."

House Permanent Select Committee on Intelligence

The House Permanent Select Committee on Intelligence Subcommittee on Intelligence Policy argues in the following viewpoint that Iran has shown no evidence that it is developing nuclear power for peaceful purposes. The author explains that Iran has not provided information about its nuclear program to the international community—and if Iran was developing nuclear power strictly for electricity, there would be no need to hide it. The author says it is also unlikely that Iran is developing nuclear power plants, because it does not have enough uranium supplies to fuel even a single nuclear reactor. Furthermore, Iran has large natural gas and oil reserves, and as such, the author questions why Iran would waste its money developing

House Permanent Select Committee on Intelligence, Subcommittee on Intelligence Policy, "Recognizing Iran as a Strategic Threat: An Intelligence Challenge for the United States," August 23, 2006.

nuclear power when it has plenty of cheap fossil fuel energy. Together, these reasons make the committee suspect Iran intends to develop nuclear technology for military purposes.

The House Permanent Select Committee on Intelligence is a committee of the United States House of Representatives. The committee oversees many executive branch departments and agencies, including the Central Intelligence Agency, Defense Intelligence Agency, Department of Homeland Security, and the National Security Agency, among many others.

AS YOU READ, CONSIDER THE FOLLOWING QUESTIONS:
1. How many tons of weapons-grade material UF6 does the author say Iran has produced? How many bombs would that be enough to make?
2. What are "uranium hemispheres," and how do they cast doubt on Iran's claim it is pursuing nuclear power for peaceful purposes?
3. If Iran sincerely wanted a peaceful nuclear power program, what does the author say it would agree to?

Iran poses a threat to the United States and its allies due to its sponsorship of terror, probable pursuit of weapons of mass destruction, and support for the insurgency in Iraq. The profile of the Iranian threat has increased over the last year [2006] due to the election of President Mahmoud Ahmadinejad, who has made public threats against the United States and Israel, the continuation of Iranian nuclear weapons research, and the recent attacks by Hezbollah, an Iranian terrorist proxy, against Israel. Iran has provided Hezbollah with financial support and weapons, including the thousands of rockets Hezbollah fired against Israel in July and August 2006. Iran thus bears significant responsibility for the recent violence in Israel and Lebanon.

Iran's efforts since December 2005 to resume enrichment of uranium, in defiance of the international community, Tehran's [Iran's capital city] willingness to endure international condemnation, isolation, and economic disruptions in order to carry out nuclear activities covertly indicates Iran is developing nuclear weapons. . . .

Iran Has a Nuclear Weapons Program

Two decades ago, Iran embarked on a secret program to acquire the capability to produce weapons-grade nuclear material. Iran has developed an extensive infrastructure, from laboratories to industrial facilities, to support its research for nuclear weapons. Producing fissile material is a complicated process and Tehran faces several key obstacles to acquiring a nuclear capability: its inability to produce or purchase fissile material, the challenges of marrying a nuclear warhead to a missile, and the difficulty of adjusting its existing missiles to carry a nuclear payload.

Since 2002, the IAEA [International Atomic Energy Agency] has issued a series of reports detailing how Iran has covertly engaged in dozens of nuclear-related activities that violate its treaty obligations to openly cooperate with the IAEA. These activities included false statements to IAEA inspectors, carrying out certain nuclear activities and experiments without notifying the IAEA, and numerous steps to deceive and mislead the IAEA. . . .

Iran Secretly Pursues Development of Nuclear Weapons

The WMD Commission (officially known as the Commission on the Intelligence of the United States Regarding Weapons of Mass Destruction) concluded in its March 2005 unclassified report that "across the board, the Intelligence Community knows disturbingly little about the nuclear programs of many of the world's most dangerous actors." American intelligence agencies do not know nearly enough about Iran's nuclear weapons program. However, based on what is known about Iranian behavior and Iranian deception efforts, the U.S. Intelligence Community assesses that Iran is intent on developing a nuclear weapons capability. Publicly available information also leads to the conclusion

FAST FACT

The International Atomic Energy Agency discovered in February 2009 that Iran has one-third more bomb-quality enriched uranium than it had previously disclosed.

that Iran has a nuclear weapons program, especially taking into account the following facts:

- Iran has covertly pursued two parallel enrichment programs—a laser process based on Russian technology and a centrifuge process. The Russian government terminated cooperation with Iran on laser enrichment in 2001, following extensive consultations with the United States, and it appears to be no longer active.
- In February 2004, Iran admitted to obtaining uranium centrifuge technology on the black market shortly after Dr. A.Q. Khan, the father of Pakistan's nuclear weapons program, confessed to secretly providing this technology to Iran, Libya, and North Korea. Khan also sold nuclear bomb plans to Libya. It is not known whether Khan sold nuclear weapon plans to Iran.
- The IAEA reported on February 27, 2006 that Iran has produced approximately 85 tons of uranium hexafluoride (UF6). If enriched through centrifuges to weapons-grade material—a capability Iran is working hard to master—this would be enough for 12 nuclear bombs.
- To produce plutonium, Iran has built a heavy water production plant and is constructing a large, heavy water–moderated reactor whose technical characteristics are well-suited for the production of weapons-grade plutonium. In support of this effort, Iran admitted in October 2003 to secretly producing small quantities of plutonium without notifying the IAEA, a violation of its treaty obligations.
- The IAEA has discovered documentation in Iran for casting and machining enriched uranium hemispheres, which are directly relevant to production of nuclear weapons components. The IAEA is also pursuing information on nuclear-related high-explosive tests and the design of a delivery system, both of which point to a military rather than peaceful purpose of the Iranian nuclear program.
- The IAEA discovered evidence in September 2003 that Iran had covertly produced the short-lived radioactive element polonium 210 (Po-210), a substance with two known uses: a neutron source for a nuclear weapon and satellite batteries. Iran told the IAEA that the polonium 210 was produced for satellite batteries but could not produce evidence for this explanation. The IAEA found

Iran's explanation about its polonium experiments difficult to believe, stating in a September 2004 report that "it remains, however, somewhat uncertain regarding the plausibility of the stated purpose of the experiments given the very limited applications of short lived Po-210 sources." . . .

Iran's Nuclear Program Is Not for Electricity

Iran has engaged in an extensive campaign to conceal from the IAEA and the world the true nature of its nuclear program.

- Iran claims that its nuclear program is peaceful and for civilian electricity. While there are differences among some experts as to whether Iran may have an interest in a civilian nuclear program in addition to a weapons program, recent findings by the Department of Energy make a convincing case that the Iranian nuclear program is inconsistent with the Iranian Government's stated purpose of developing civil nuclear power in order to achieve energy independence. Iran's claims that its nuclear program is peaceful also is belied by its record of non-cooperation

Those who are suspicious of Iran's nuclear intentions point to the country's abundant gas and oil reserves that are much cheaper sources of energy than expensive nuclear power.

with the IAEA, its decision to pursue nuclear technology covertly, and the fact that Iran does not have enough indigenous uranium resources to fuel even one power-generating reactor over its lifetime, although it does have enough uranium to make several nuclear bombs.

- Aside from Iran's lack of uranium deposits, Iran's claim that its nuclear program is for electricity production appears doubtful in light of its large oil and natural gas reserves. Iran's natural gas reserves are the second largest in the world and the energy industry estimates that Iran flares enough natural gas annually to generate electricity equivalent to the output of four . . . reactors. . . .
- Furthermore, there is no rational reason for Iran to pursue a peaceful nuclear program in secret and risk international sanctions when the International Atomic Energy Agency encourages and assists peaceful nuclear programs. If Iran sincerely wanted a peaceful nuclear program, the IAEA would have helped it develop one provided that Tehran agreed to IAEA supervision and monitoring.

Iran Hides Its Nuclear Activities

In an October 1, 2003 agreement with the EU-3,[1] Iran pledged "to engage in full cooperation with the IAEA to address and resolve through full transparency all requirements and outstanding issues of the Agency." In spite of this, Iran has admitted to conducting certain nuclear activities to IAEA inspectors only after the IAEA presented it with clear evidence or asked Tehran to correct prior explanations that were inaccurate, implausible, or fraught with contradictions. Iran's admissions have been grudging and piecemeal, and its cooperation with IAEA inspectors has been accompanied by protests, accusations, and threats. Iran's recalcitrant behavior toward IAEA inspections drove IAEA Director Mohammed ElBaradei to declare in a November 2003 report:

> The recent disclosures by Iran about its nuclear program clearly show that, in the past, Iran had concealed many aspects of its nuclear activities, with resultant breaches of its obligation to comply with the provisions of the Safeguards Agreement. Iran's policy

1. EU-3 refers to the United Kingdom, France, and Germany and these nations' attempts to end Iran's nuclear program.

Iran Has No Need for Nuclear Energy

Government officials doubt Iran's claim that it wants nuclear technology for peaceful energy purposes because it has large domestic reserves of oil and natural gas.

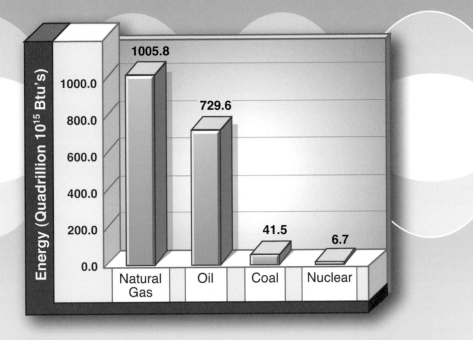

Taken from: "Recognizing Iran as a Strategic Threat: An Intelligence Challenge for the United States," Staff Report of the House Permanent Committee on Intelligence, Subcommittee on Intelligence Policy, August 23, 2006.

of concealment continued until last month, with co-operation being limited and reactive, and information being slow in coming, changing and contradictory.

More Definitive Intelligence Needed

Although it is likely that Iran is pursuing nuclear weapons, there is the possibility that Iran could be engaged in a denial and deception campaign to exaggerate progress on its nuclear program such as Saddam Hussein apparently did concerning his WMD programs. U.S. leaders need more definitive intelligence to judge the status of the Iranian nuclear program and whether there have been any related deception efforts.

While not an instance of Iranian perfidy [deliberate breach of faith], the spring 2006 decision by IAEA Director General ElBaradei to remove Mr. Christopher Charlier, the chief IAEA Iran inspector, for allegedly raising concerns about Iranian deception regarding its nuclear program and concluding that the purpose of Iran's nuclear program is to construct weapons, should give U.S. policymakers great pause. The United States has entrusted the IAEA with providing a truly objective assessment of Iran's nuclear program. IAEA officials should not hesitate to conclude that the purpose of the Iranian nuclear program is to produce weapons if that is where the evidence leads. If Mr. Charlier was removed for not adhering to an unstated IAEA policy barring IAEA officials from telling the whole truth about the Iranian nuclear program, the United States and the international community have a serious problem on their hands.

EVALUATING THE AUTHOR'S ARGUMENTS:

In this viewpoint the author argues that Iran's secrecy about its nuclear power program indicates that Iran intends to use its nuclear power for military purposes. What do you think? If Iran was developing nuclear power for peaceful purposes, is there any reason it would want to remain secretive about its program? Are there any other reasons why Iran might not want to divulge information about its nuclear program to the international community? Explain your position and whether you think Iran should be allowed to have nuclear technology.

Facts About Nuclear Power

Editor's note: These facts can be used in reports or papers to reinforce or add credibility when making important points or claims.

Nuclear Power in the United States

According to the U.S. Department of Energy:
- Nuclear power provides for 8.5 percent of America's total energy needs.
- There are 104 nuclear reactors in sixty-six power plants in the United States.
- The United States uses two types of nuclear power plants: boiling water reactors (BWR) and pressurized water reactors (PWR).
- Approximately 70 percent of nuclear reactors in the United States are PWRs.

The Nuclear Regulatory Commission (NRC) must approve construction and operational plans before a nuclear power plant can be built in the United States.

The Office of Nuclear Energy provides the following facts about nuclear energy in the United States:
- Nuclear power plants in the United States are designed to operate safely for up to forty years.
- One hundred sixty-one million Americans live within seventy-five miles of nuclear waste.
- High-level radioactive nuclear waste is stored in 125 sites in thirty-nine states in the United States.
- Debates have raged for decades over whether Yucca Mountain in Nevada should become the first permanent nuclear waste storage depository.
- On March 28, 1979, a nuclear reactor at Three Mile Island malfunctioned, causing one-half of the core to melt. Severe core meltdown is considered the most dangerous nuclear plant malfunction.

- Each year in the United States, nuclear power plants produce as much energy as that used by California, Texas, and New York combined.

According to the Energy Information Administration:
- Thirty-one states in the United States have nuclear power plants.
- The largest nuclear power plant in the United States is in Palo Verde, Arizona.
- Illinois has the most nuclear reactors of any state—six.
- Pennsylvania has the second-highest number of nuclear reactors—five.
- The first commercial nuclear power plant opened in Shippingport, Pennsylvania, in 1957. The plant was decommissioned during President Ronald Reagan's first term in 1982.
- In 1955 Arco, Idaho, became the first town to rely on nuclear power to provide electricity to its entire community.
- The United States produced 3,922,823 pounds of uranium concentrate in 2008.

Nuclear Power Around the World
According to the Energy Information Administration:
- There are 446 nuclear power plants worldwide.
- The first electricity from nuclear power was generated in 1954 at the Obninsk Nuclear Power Plant in the former Soviet Union.
- The United States has the most nuclear reactors in the world.
- Great Britain's nuclear reactors have been in use longer than any other nation's.
- France has the four largest nuclear reactors.
- Nuclear power–produced electricity is expected to increase from about 2.6 trillion kilowatt-hours in 2005 to 3.8 trillion kilowatt-hours in 2030.

According to the International Energy Agency:
- There are more than fifty nuclear power plants in France, producing 79 percent of that country's electricity.
- Australia does not produce any nuclear energy.
- As of 2005 China had just eleven nuclear reactors that produced only 1 percent of its electricity.

- India derives 1 percent of its electricity from nuclear power.
- Iran began plans for building a nuclear reactor in Bushehr in 1974.
- Six percent of energy produced in Russia was generated by nuclear power in 2005.
- In 2006, 12 percent of Germany's electricity was generated by nuclear power.
- Germany plans to shut down all of its nuclear power plants by 2020.

According to a 2008 report in the *Guardian*, 20 percent of Great Britain's electricity is supplied by nuclear power.

Science Friday states the following facts about nuclear power plants around the world:
- Fifty percent of Ukraine's energy is from nuclear power plants.
- China plans to build forty new reactors by 2020.

On April 26, 1986, the world's worst nuclear power plant accident occurred at the Chernobyl plant in what is now Ukraine. An explosion caused a fire that burned for ten days, sending radioactive material into the atmosphere that spread across the former Soviet Union and Europe.

According to the World Nuclear Association:
- Demand for electricity is expected to double between 2004 and 2030.
- Fifteen percent of the word's electricity is generated by nuclear power.
- Thirty-four percent of electricity in the European Union is produced by nuclear power.
- Seventy percent of increased energy demand is from developing countries, such as China and India.

Nuclear Power and Weapons of Mass Destruction

In February 2005 FBI director Robert Mueller testified before the Select Committee on U.S. Intelligence before the Senate that nuclear power plants were al Qaeda terrorist targets.

According to a fact sheet published by the Nuclear Information and Resource Service:
- The Callaway reactor at the Missouri nuclear power plant produces enough plutonium in one year to create forty nuclear bombs.
- If the Callaway plant continues to operate for thirty years, it will produce enough plutonium to make twelve hundred nuclear bombs.

On September 19, 2006, Al Gore said, "During my 8 years in the White House, every nuclear weapons proliferation issue we dealt with was connected to a nuclear reactor program."

According to Green America, there are at least eight ways to cause a severe meltdown at a nuclear power plant.

Nuclear Power Versus Other Energy Sources
According to Nuclear Info.net:
- Natural gas produces between 40 and 50 percent less CO_2 emissions than coal.
- Fourth-generation nuclear reactors set to become operational by 2020 will be fifty times more efficient than the second-generation reactors currently in use.
- Because of changing weather patterns, wind energy produces 25 to 35 percent of its top capacity when averaged out over a year.
- Electricity from wind power is the fastest-growing renewable energy program in Australia.

According to the Department of the Interior:
- Twenty-one million acres of land in the United States have wind energy potential.
- Twenty-nine million acres of land in the United States have solar energy potential.
- One hundred forty million acres of land in Alaska have geothermal energy potential.

According to the Environmental Protection Agency:
- Renewable energy and nuclear power each supply less than nine percent of the nation's total energy.

- Nuclear energy does not produce the greenhouse gases carbon dioxide, sulfur dioxide, or nitrogen oxides.
- Nuclear power plants must shut down every eighteen to twenty-four months to replace uranium fuel. The used fuel then becomes radioactive waste.
- Nuclear power plants in the United States produce 2,000 metric tons of radioactive waste.
- Approximately twenty percent of electricity in the United States is generated by nuclear power.
- Nearly 50 percent of electricity in the United States is generated by coal.
- Gas generates approximately 19 percent of electricity used in the United States.
- Slightly more than 3 percent of electricity used in the United States is produced by oil.
- Wind power is responsible for less than one-half of 1 percent of electricity used in the United States.
- Solar power produces 0.01 percent of electricity used in the United States.

Glossary

Atom: The basic building block of all matter. Atoms are the smallest particles of an element. They consist of a central core called the nucleus, which is made up of protons and neutrons. Electrons revolve in orbits in the region surrounding the nucleus.

Dry-cask storage: A method for storing spent fuel. This method employs large, durable containers made of steel or reinforced concrete. They are usually 18 or more inches thick. Instead of water, casks use steel, concrete, or lead to shield radiation.

Fission: The splitting of atoms that causes large amounts of energy to be released.

Fossil fuel: An energy source that formed over the course of millions of years from biological decay. Examples include coal, oil, and natural gas.

Fuel assembly: Assemblies of fuel rods that are placed in a nuclear reactor vessel to form the "core." A fuel assembly may contain 60 to 300 fuel rods.

Fuel pellets: Small ceramic cylinders that hold uranium fuel used in nuclear reactors.

Fuel rod: A long, slender tube that holds the fuel pellets.

Greenhouse gases: Substances such as carbon dioxide (CO_2) that are released by the burning of fossil fuels. Some believe that an increase in greenhouse gases in the atmosphere is causing climate change.

Megawatt: A measure of electric power equal to one million watts.

Nuclear power: Energy in the form of heat or electricity that has been produced by the process of nuclear fission within a nuclear reactor.

Nuclear Regulatory Commission (NRC): A U.S. agency charged with developing and administering rules for regulating activities relating to nuclear power.

Radiation: Particles or rays emitted from the nucleus of an unstable radioactive atom as a result of radioactive decay. At high doses these can be lethal.

Radioactivity: The spontaneous transformation, decay, or disintegration of an unstable atom.

Reactor vessel: A device in which nuclear fission may be sustained and controlled. A nuclear reactor vessel houses the core (made up of fuel rods and other instruments) of most types of power reactors.

Renewable energy: Energy derived from sources such as the sun, wind, or water. These are considered renewable because there is an unending supply of wind, sunlight, and wave activity.

Spent fuel: Fuel rods that no longer have enough fissionable uranium in them to make energy.

Uranium: A naturally radioactive and very dense element from which nuclear power is generated.

Organizations to Contact

The editors have compiled the following list of organizations concerned with the issues debated in this book. The descriptions are derived from materials provided by the organizations. All have publications or information available for interested readers. The list was compiled on the date of publication of the present volume; the information provided here may change. Be aware that many organizations take several weeks or longer to respond to queries, so allow as much time as possible.

American Nuclear Society
555 North Kensington Ave.
La Grange Park, IL 60526
(800) 323-3044
Web site: www.new.ans.org

The American Nuclear Society was established in 1954 to promote the understanding of nuclear science and technology. The organization is made up of eleven thousand scientists, educators, and other professionals that are committed to unifying those working in nuclear technologies. The American Nuclear Society publishes the journals *Nuclear Science and Engineering, Nuclear News, Fusion Science and Technology,* and *Radwaste Solutions.*

Energy Information Association (EIA)
1000 Independence Ave. SW
Washington, DC 20585
(202) 586-8800
e-mail: infoCtr@eia.doe.gov
Web site: www.eia.doe.gov

The EIA provides data and analyses to assist in energy policy making. The EIA also seeks to increase public understanding of energy production, including nuclear power. It collects data and analyzes energy markets, trading, and supply and demand as well as importing and exporting of energy sources. The EIA is divided into four programs that study various energy-related topics.

Green America (GA)
1612 K St. NW, Ste. 600
Washington, DC 20006
(800) 584-7336
Web site: www.coopamerica.org

GA (formerly known as Co-op America) was founded in 1982. GA is opposed to the use of nuclear power and takes issue with it as a means to attack global warming. Its Web site includes a list of ten reasons why nuclear power is not the answer to global energy and environmental concerns. Some reasons GA is against nuclear power include nuclear waste toxicity, danger of nuclear proliferation, threat to national security, risk of accidents, risk of cancer from radiation, and others. GA produces several publications, including *National Green Pages, Real Green, Green American,* and *Guide to Socially Responsible Investing.*

Greenpeace
702 H St. NW, Ste. 300
Washington, DC 20001
(202) 462-1177
e-mail: info@wdc.greenpeace.org
Web site: www.greenpeace.org

Greenpeace was formed in 1971 when a small group of activists chartered a fishing boat and set off to protest nuclear testing off the coast of Alaska. The organization continues to stage peaceful protests against the use of nuclear power while standing up for renewable energy sources. Greenpeace asserts that nuclear power is a dangerous distraction from true solutions to increasing demand for energy and worsening global warming. Greenpeace seeks to educate policy makers and the international public by publishing annual reports and fact sheets on global warming and nuclear energy.

International Atomic Energy Agency (IAEA)
PO Box 100, Wagramer Strasse 5
A-1400 Vienna, Austria

e-mail: Official.Mail@iaea.org
Web site: www.iaea.or.at

The IAEA was established in 1957 with help from the United Nations as an international "Atoms for Peace" organization. The IAEA works with its members to promote the safe and peaceful use of nuclear technologies. The IAEA has offices in Vienna, Geneva, New York City, Toronto, and Tokyo that employ more than twenty-two hundred staff members in ninety countries to ensure that nuclear power and technology policy making include safety and security, safeguards and verification, and the promotion of nuclear science. The IAEA makes annual reports to the United Nations General Assembly and Security Council on matters of international peace and safety. The IAEA publishes several scientific journals and papers, including *Effective Nuclear Regulatory Systems: Facing Safety and Security Challenges* and *Innovative and Adaptive Technologies in Decommissioning of Nuclear Facilities.*

International Radiation Protection Association (IRPA)
28 rue de la Redoute, 92260
Fontenay-aux-Roses, France
Web site: www.irpa.net/index.php?option=com_frontpage&Itemid=1

The IRPA provides support and protection to people and the environment from the hazards of radiation. Every four years the International Congress of IRPA meets to discuss the safety of medical, scientific, and industrial radiological practices. The theme of the 2012 International Congress of IRPA is Living with Radiation—Engaging with Society.

Nuclear Energy Institute (NEI)
1776 I St. NW, Ste. 400
Washington, DC 20006-3708
(202) 739-8000
e-mail: media@nei.org
Web site: www.nei.org

The NEI is the policy organization for the nuclear energy and technology industry. The NEI works both within the United States and globally to form policies that further the use of nuclear technology and energy around the world. Members include more than three hundred corporations in fifteen countries that work together to promote the safe use of nuclear power to generate electricity as well as the relicensing of nuclear power plants currently in operation. The NEI publishes *Nuclear Energy Insight, Nuclear Policy Outlook, Perspective on Public Opinion,* and *Nuclear Performance Monthly.*

Nuclear Information and Resource Service (NIRS)
6930 Carroll Ave., Ste. 340
Takoma Park, MD 20912
(301) 270-6477
e-mail: nirsnet@nirs.org
Web site: www.nirs.org/home.htm

The NIRS formed in the 1970s to educate the public on the dangers of nuclear energy and technology. It has expanded to become a global watchdog group that adamantly opposes the construction of new nuclear power plants. The NIRS organizes protests and campaigns against using nuclear energy. It also seeks to change global energy policies to focus on renewable sources such as wind and solar power.

Office of Nuclear Energy
1000 Independence Ave. SW
Washington, DC 20585
(800) 342-5363
Web site: www.ne.doe.gov

The Office of Nuclear Energy is a department within the U.S. Department of Energy that focuses on promoting nuclear power in the United States. Its mission is to encourage the Department of Energy to invest in the development of nuclear science and technology and to develop new nuclear energy technologies. It also seeks to develop proliferation-resistant nuclear fuel and to maintain national nuclear facilities. The organization offers free e-mail updates for subscribers to *Nuclear Power 2010, Gen IV, Next Generation Nuclear Plant,* and *University Funding.*

Radiation Information Network (RIN)
Department of Health Physics
Idaho State University, Campus Box 8106
Pocatello, ID 83209
(208) 282-4308
Web site: www.physics.isu.edu/radinf

The RIN is run by professors and students within the Department of Health Physics at Idaho State University. It collects the latest research and information about radiation for those who work in the radiation protection industry as well as for anyone interested in learning more about its effects. The RIN seeks to educate the public about regulatory and professional information regarding radiation.

World Nuclear Association (WNA)
22a Saint James's Square
London, SW1Y 4JH United Kingdom
44 (0)20 7451 1520
e-mail: wna@world-nuclear.org
Web site: www.world-nuclear.org/info/info.htm

The WNA is a private, international organization committed to the peaceful use of nuclear power. It believes nuclear power is a sustainable solution to global energy needs and is interested in furthering nuclear technologies and education. The WNA publishes papers on nuclear fuel production, industry economics, trade issues, radiological safety, transporting nuclear materials, decommissioning nuclear power plants, handling radioactive waste, sustainability of nuclear energy, security, and safety. The WNA also publishes the brochure *World Nuclear Association: Vision in Action.*

World Wildlife Federation (WWF)
1250 Twenty-fourth St. NW
Washington, DC 20585
(202) 293-4800
Web site: www.panda.org

The WWF was started in 1961 by a few concerned world citizens and has since grown into one of the world's largest environmental organizations. The WWF has more than thirteen hundred conservation projects around the world. It is seriously concerned with the threat nuclear energy and technology pose to humans, animals, and the environment. The WWF is adamantly opposed to nuclear power, believing it poses serious security risks and will distract from creating innovative clean energy alternatives. The WWF includes the following downloadable publications on its Web site: *WWF Position Statement on Nuclear*

Power, Full Report on Climate Change and Nuclear Power, and *Climate Solutions: WWF's Vision for 2050.*

Yucca Mountain Information Office
PO Box 990
Eureka, NV 89316
(775) 237-5707
e-mail: ecyucca@eurekanv.org
Web site: www.yuccamountain.org

The Eureka County local government started this organization to keep its residents apprised of the history and current developments with the Yucca Mountain Depository project. Residents of Eureka and other interested parties can follow the progression of the controversial proposed permanent nuclear waste dump with the information provided by the Yucca Mountain Information Office. Tools offered to the public include a time line, maps, litigation information, and a quarterly newsletter.

For Further Reading

Books

Bodansky, David. *Nuclear Energy: Principles, Practices, and Prospects.* New York: Springer, 2008. Presents a case for using nuclear energy and explains the components of nuclear power.

Caldicott, Helen. *Nuclear Power Is Not the Answer.* New York: New Press, 2007. Refutes claims that nuclear power is a safe and clean energy alternative.

Cravens, Gwyneth. *Power to Save the World: The Truth About Nuclear Energy.* London: Vintage, 2008. Argues that nuclear power is the only large-scale electricity source alternative.

Herbst, Alan M. *Nuclear Energy Now: Why the Time Has Come for the World's Most Misunderstood Energy Source.* Hoboken, NJ: Wiley, 2007. Debunks misconceptions about the dangers of nuclear power and explains why it is the best energy option.

Hore-Lacy, Ian. *Nuclear Energy in the Twenty-first Century.* Burlington, MA: Academic, 2006. Discusses current and future energy demands and explains how nuclear power can meet them.

Makhijani, Arjun. *Carbon-Free and Nuclear-Free: A Roadmap for U.S. Energy Policy.* Muskegon, MI: RDR, 2007. Argues that the United States must lead the world away from its reliance on nuclear power and toward achieving zero CO_2 emissions.

Ramsey, Charles B. *Commercial Nuclear Power: Assuring Safety for the Future.* Charleston, SC: BookSurge, 2006. Describes how nuclear energy meets current and future energy needs.

Smith, Brice. *Insurmountable Risks: The Dangers of Using Nuclear Power to Combat Global Climate Change.* Muskegon, MI: RDR, 2006. Explains why using nuclear power to combat global warming is too risky to consider.

Sweet, William. *Kicking the Carbon Habit: Global Warming and the Case for Renewable and Nuclear Energy.* New York: Columbia

University Press, 2003. Assesses the benefits of switching to predominantly nuclear- and wind-generated energy sources.

Tucker, William. *Terrestrial Energy: How Nuclear Energy Will Lead the Green Revolution and End America's Energy Odyssey.* Savage, MD: Bartleby, 2008. Examines the pros and cons of various energy sources and concludes that nuclear power is America's cleanest and most efficient option.

Periodicals and Internet Sources

Alvarez, Robert. "Nuclear Recycling Fails the Test," *Foreign Policy in Focus*, July 7, 2008. www.fpif.org/fpiftxt/5351.

Baker, Peter, and Dafna Linzer. "Nuclear Energy Plan Would Use Spent Fuel," *Washington Post*, January 26, 2006. www.washington post.com/wp-dyn/content/article/2006/01/25/AR2006012502229 .html.

Clayton, Mark. "How Green Is Nuclear Power?" *Christian Science Monitor*, March 7, 2007. www.csmonitor.com/2007/0307/ p01s04-sten.html.

Coopersmith, Jonathan. "Nuclear Waste in Space?" *Space Review*, August 22, 2005. www.thespacereview.com/article/437/1.

Dudziak, Donald J. "Spent Fuel Rods Are Not Waste," *Albuquerque Journal*, April 4, 2007. www.abqjournal.com/opinion/guest_ columns/551837opinion04-04-07.htm.

Dunn, Philip. "Safe Nuclear Power and Green Hydrogen Fuel," *PhysOrg.com*, December 11, 2005. www.physorg.com/news8956 .html.

Ferguson, Charles, and Sharon Squassoni. "Why Nuclear Energy Isn't the Great Green Hope," *Foreign Policy*, June 2007. www.foreign policy.com/story/cms.php?story_id=3896.

Fischer, Seth. "Nuking Nuclear Waste," *Popular Science*, April 23, 2007. www.popsci.com/scitech/article/2007-04/nuking-nuclear-waste.

Garber, Kent. "Some Nuclear Energy Backers Say Uranium Could Be Magic Bullet," *U.S. News & World Report*, October 14, 2008. www.usnews.com/articles/news/2008/10/14/some-nuclear-energy-backers-say-uranium-alternative-could-be-a-magic-bullet.html.

Gelinas, Nicole. "Nuclear Power: The Investment Outlook," *Energy Policy and the Environment Report*, June 2007. www.manhattan-institute.org/pdf/eper_01.pdf.

Hannum, William H., Gerald E. Marsh, and George S. Stanford. "Smarter Use of Nuclear Waste," *Scientific American*, December 2005. www.nationalcenter.org/NuclearFastReactorsSA1205.pdf.

Harsanyi, David. "The Greening of Nuclear Power," *Denver Post*, January 27, 2008. www.denverpost.com/opinion/ci_8070598.

Holt, Mark, and Anthony Andrews. "Report—Congressional Research Service—Nuclear Power Plants and Terrorism," Carnegie Endowment for International Peace, August 8, 2008. www.carnegie endowment.org/publications/index.cfm?fa=view&id=19760&prog =zgp&proj=znpp.

Johnston, Rob. "Ten Myths About Nuclear Power," *Spiked*, January 9, 2008. www.spiked-online.com/index.php?/site/article/4259.

Kleiner, Kurt. "Nuclear Energy: Assessing the Emissions," *Nature*, September 24, 2008. www.nature.com/climate/2008/0810/full/ climate.2008.99.html.

Lewis, Judith. "The Nuclear Option: So You're Against Nuclear Power. Do You Know Why?" *Mother Jones*, May–June 2008. www .motherjones.com/cgi-bin/print_article.pl?url=http://www.mother jones.com/news/feature/2008/05/the-nuclear-option-2.html.

Madsen, Travis, and Johanna Neumann. "Powering Maryland's Future: How Clean Energy Outperforms Nuclear Power in Delivering a Reliable, Safe and Affordable Supply of Electricity," Maryland PIRG Foundation, July 2008. www.uspirg.org/uploads/ cQ/v3/cQv31JoZJ7bnDGiI9lllcg/Powering-Marylands-Future .pdf.

Moore, Patrick. "Going Nuclear: A Green Makes the Case," *Washington Post*, April 16, 2006. www.washingtonpost.com/wp-dyn/content/ article/2006/04/14/AR2006041401209.html.

Noel, Mike, and Brad Daw. "Nuclear Power Is Safe and Clean," *Deseret News*, February 13, 2006. http://deseretnews.com/article/content/mobile/1,5620,635183809,00.html.

Nuclear Energy Institute. "Nuclear Energy Plays Essential Role In Reducing Greenhouse Gas Emissions," July 2008. www.nei.org/filefolder/Nuclear_Energy_Plays_Essential_Role_in_Reducing_Greenhouse_Gas_Emissions_0708.pdf.

Petit, Charles. "Nuclear Power—Risking a Comeback," *National Geographic*, August 2006. http://science.nationalgeographic.com/science/space/universe/nuclear-comeback.html.

Slater, Alice. "Nuclear Power No Solution to Global Warming," *Pacific Ecologist*, Winter, 2008. www.wagingpeace.org/articles/2008/08/18_slater_towards_irena.pdf.

Spencer, Jack. "Finland's Rational Approach to Nuclear Power," *World & I Online*, June 2008. www.worldandi.com/subscribers/feature_detail.asp?num=26271.

———. "Recycling Nuclear Fuel: The French Do It, Why Can't Oui?" Heritage Foundation, December 28, 2007. www.heritage.org/Press/Commentary/ed010108d.cfm.

Spencer, Jack, and Nicolas Loris. "Critics of Nuclear Power's Costs Miss the Point," Heritage Foundation Web Memo No. 1961, June 18, 2008. www.heritage.org/Research/EnergyandEnvironment/upload/wm_1961.pdf.

———. "Dispelling Myths About Nuclear Energy," Heritage Foundation, December 3, 2007. www.heritage.org/Research/EnergyandEnvironment/upload/bg_2087.pdf.

Tampa Bay Online. "Nuclear Power Offers Clean Energy, Clean Air," May 30, 2007. www.tbo.com/news/opinion/commentary/MGB38I8ZA2F.html.

Union of Concerned Scientists. "Reprocessing and Nuclear Terrorism," 2008. www.ucsusa.org/nuclear_power/nuclear_power_risk/nuclear_proliferation_and_terrorism/reprocessing-and-nuclear.html.

Walsh, Brian. "Is Nuclear Power Viable?" *Time*, June 6, 2008. www.time.com/time/health/article/0,8599,1812540,00.html.

Wenzel, Elsa. "Nuke Power Not So Green or Clean," CNET.com, June 11, 2007. http://news.com.com/Nuke+power+not+so+clean+or+green/2008-11392_3-6189817.html?tag=st.num.

Whadcock, Ian. "Life After Death: Nuclear Power Is Clean, but Can It Overcome Its Image Problem?" *Economist*, June 19, 2008. www.economist.com/specialreports/displaystory.cfm?story_id=11565609.

Web Sites

Energy Kids Page (www.eia.doe.gov/kids/index.html). The Energy Kids Page was started by the Energy Information Association to teach kids about different energy sources. The site uses historical references, facts, games, and classroom activities to explain high-level energy concepts such as nuclear fusion.

Energy Quest (www.energyquest.ca.gov/story/chapter13.html). The California Energy Commission designed this award-winning educational Web site to explain energy and conservation to students of all ages. Chapter 13 explains what nuclear energy is and how fission and fusion occur.

Federal Energy Regulatory Commission (FERC) Student's Corner (www.ferc.gov/students/index.htm). FERC is an independent governmental commission that is organized within the Department of Energy. It designed this Web site to help students understand how energy is regulated in the United States.

General Atomics Fusion Education (http://fusioned.gat.com). This Web site was created by the General Atomics Energy Group to assist teachers and students in understanding how nuclear solutions can meet global energy needs.

Kids and Energy (www.kids.esdb.bg/uranium.html). The Kids and Energy Web site uses photos, graphs, and games to explain how nuclear power plants generate energy. In addition, the site provides facts about conservation and renewable energy sources.

Nuclear Power Now (www.nuclearnow.org). This Web site seeks to educate American citizens and government officials on the benefits of using nuclear power. It provides information and statistics on nuclear energy technology, economics, safety, politics, and laws.

United States Department of Energy for Students and Kids (www
.energy.gov/forstudentsandkids.htm). The U.S. Department of
Energy for Students and Kids provides facts, glossaries, time lines,
and other easy-to-understand materials to explain high-energy
physics such as nuclear power.

**United States Nuclear Regulatory Commission (NRC) Student's
Corner** (www.nrc.gov/reading-rm/basic-ref/students.html). The
NRC created the Student's Corner to explain all aspects of nuclear energy. Topics include nuclear reactors, radiation, decommissioning reactors, security issues, emergency planning, and nuclear
waste.

Index

Nuclear power plants
  are not vulnerable to terrorist
    attacks, 96–102
  are vulnerable to terrorist
    attack, 91–95
  construction of, 77, 84
  improved air quality and,
    14
  in Iran, 107
  lack of safety standards for,
    20–21
  in New York, *13*
  safety and operational
    failures at, 55
  security at, 97–101
  subsidies for, 22
  water consumption by, 49
  worldwide, 15
Nuclear radiation, 53–54, 56,
  58–62, 85
Nuclear reactors, 33, 87, 88
Nuclear Regulatory
  Commission (NRC),
  93–95, 97, 101
Nuclear waste
  can be recycled, 76–82
  can be safely contained,
    65–68
  cannot be recycled safely,
    83–89
  cannot be safely contained,
    69–75
  current amount of, 63, 73
  danger from, 18–22
  decay of, 70–72
  disposal of, 48, 63, 78

generation of, 8, 21, 48
  misleading notions about,14
  reprocessing of, 62–63,
    92–93
  transportation of, *71*, 73,
    93–95, 101
  U.S. policy on, 78–79
Nuclear Waste Policy Act, 78
Nuclear weapons program, in
  Iran, 111–116
Nuclear weapons proliferation,
  99–101

O
Obama, Barack, 70
Ozone, 14

P
Pakistan, 108
Particulate pollution, 14
Pimentel, David, 39
Plutonium
  decay life of, 67
  Iranian production of, 112
  reduction in amount of, 63
  reprocessing of, 67, 84,
    87–88, 92–93
Pollution
  air, 14, 18
  from nuclear power, 17–22,
    85
  See also Nuclear waste
Polonium, 112–113
Population growth, 24
Powell, James, 41
Pueblo Indians, 19

Picture Credits

Maury Aaseng, 15, 19, 27, 33, 42, 47, 48, 55, 61, 78–79, 100, 107, 115

Image copyright haak78, 2009. Used under license from Shutterstock
.com, 10

AP Images, 13, 21, 46, 50, 53, 62, 67, 71, 85, 94, 98, 105, 113

© A.T. Willett/Alamy, 25

© G P Bowater/Alamy, 34

© Ken Welsh/Alamy, 39

Lucas Schifres/*Bloomberg News*/Landov, 80

Robert Sorbo/Reuters/Landov, 90